Drive Me Wild

A Western Odyssey

Christina Nealson

The CreateSpace Edition of a
Wildwords Publication

Drive Me Wild
A Western Odyssey

*****

Credits

Cover photos by Christina Nealson
www.christinanealson.com

Formatting and cover design by Debora Lewis
www.arenapublishing.org

Editing by Harvey Stanbrough
www.harveystanbrough.com

*****

ISBN-13: 978-1478291350

ISBN-10: 1478291354

1-19-13

for Mothers of the earth, sea and sky

*to Bonnie —
for the
wild
heart —
Christina*

Metaphorically, the seeker of truth has to be a person without a place, always on the road, peripatetic, and if the seeker wants instead to take up residence, to feel secure, then the truth turns into lies.

Robert Sardello

And, now, the moment. A moment such as this is unique. To be sure, it is short and temporal, as the moment is; it is passing, as the moment is, past, as the moment is in the next moment, and yet it is decisive, and yet it is filled with the eternal. A moment such as this must have a special name. Let us call it: the fullness of time.

Soren Kierkegaard

Go!

Aunt Clara

Odyssey: a long wandering or voyage usually marked by many changes of fortune; an intellectual or spiritual wandering or quest.

Introduction

Last night I dreamt I was in a dance hall with a bunch of dowdy women. Their curdled legs adorned in baggy shorts and cowboy boots, we were line dancing to "Elvira." I could still hear the music when I opened my eyes. I rolled over and faced the velvety red rose and a yellow candle I had placed on the side table the night before. I smiled in the moment as I remembered I was sleeping alone. Jay had driven to Denver for book tour. The queen-sized bed in the 7X10 motorhome bedroom was mine. All mine.

The melodious trill of a yellow warbler punctuated the rush of the nearby stream. I stretched into the morning as Pooka uncurled herself from the crotch of my bent leg and hopped across the bed. She turned back to me and gave me "the look." I obeyed, which is what one does in the presence of a Bengal cat. I kicked the comforter away, made my way through the narrow nipple-polisher hallway and let her outside. I ignored the dog, whose morning ritual included a piece of bread with peanut butter. I bee-lined it back to bed, lit that yellow candle and sank into birdsong.

It came softly at first... the distant droll of a diesel pickup, building from loud to louder as it turned down my graveled dead-end street. What the—It was 6:15 in the *morning*. Saturday. The contractors arrived one by one. An army of worker ants in their testosterone-mobiles, readying the site for the cement truck soon to follow.

I did the only thing I could do, short of pulling out my .357 Ruger and firing away. I cranked up Mozart's "String Duos and Trios," made my morning espresso and created my own ruckus: I ran the vacuum cleaner over the little patch of rug.

1

It couldn't have been more outlandish. I abhorred the metal monstrosities, yet there I was, soul-pushed up two narrow steps to tackle the thorny transition from conventional home to a spam-can with wheels, to face the excruciating liberation from 95% of my possessions while wading through the practical. How *did* a writer aka solitude junkie work out the rhythms of the day with a stubborn German husband, a shedding black Newfie and a wild-eyed leopard cat that didn't? Shed, that is.

Climb aboard, if you dare. The geographical map covers British Columbia to the tip of the Baja peninsula; the mystical map is another matter, as the dream of a drive in pianissimo crescendoed toward a deafening spiritual climax. Gray whales reached for my hand in the middle of a Baja lagoon. I wandered into the midst of four mountain lions lazing on a mountainside. A grizzly stared me down. Mothers all, with their young, they left no doubt that nature had grabbed the wheel. The journey of the soul was the answer. My life as writer, my marriage and the very essence of the wild—my own and the planet's—were the questions.

As I take my place behind the curved, un-paned window on the world, I tell you that soul is not a static venture inward, but an aerodynamic journey outward. It leaves intellect in the dust in favor of flesh, landscape and the edgy terrain of risk. My story is a potent blend of present moment and the holy unknown, a moment-to-moment awareness, of seeing and feeling deeply into the nature of things through direct experience. It speaks to a simple life, a richness not defined by money. And although many believe, as did Edith Wharton, that soul "sits alone and waits for a footstep that never comes," I beg to differ.

Joy rides take many forms; they make mincemeat of plans.

Part I

Kierkegaard and Apple Pie

One

I was over it. The serene pastures of calving cows in Taos had given way to blocks of snazzy condos. The rev of low-rider car engines drowned out rooster crows. I swore the old adobes crumbled a few more inches with every bellowing bass. The rustic charm no longer compensated for the energy it took to step outside my door. I walked at dawn and couldn't stand to watch one more drunk driver swerve to hit a dog. The word *move* grabbed me by the scruff of my neck.

It was late September. Jay and I gentled bikes along the slow-flowing Rio Grande, a narrow asphalt road that curved around ruddy rock walls and aromatic sage. The day brimmed with sightings of green-winged teal and statue-still great blues. Two golden eagles lazed upon a cliff top.

Jay pulled up beside me as a sudden headwind slowed us down. I turned to him and the words popped out of my mouth: "We're asking the wrong question! It's not *where* will we live? What if we sold the house and bought an RV? Took home with us?"

Jay lowered his sunglasses over his nose and cast a, "What have you been smoking?" look. Neither one of us had set foot in an RV. We were backpackers. The closest we came to RVs was a tent thrown into the back of the car. Now I wanted to sell the house? Trade real estate for wheel estate? We pedaled on, speechless at the revelation that had flown in on the wings of reverie; but the idea had taken root, and over the next few weeks the romance of the rubber tramp life eked its way into our lives.

Let me count the ways. We'd be free of debt, property taxes and yard work. Free to travel wherever, to explore myriad places of splendor. Time would be ours. Jay could re-visit his favorite tomes like *Moby Dick*. I pictured myself waking with the dawn to write in remote, silent places. I relished a life of spontaneity. Going down the road and turning left or right on a whim. And, our expenses would plummet.

True enough, motorhomes were at the top of my conspicuous consumption trash heap. But a few key strokes and dip into the Internet and I discovered that several million people lived their life as full-timers. Motorhome as primary residence blinked neon eco-green. Energy consumption paled next to that of heating and cooling a house. We'd opt for a rig with double paned windows and solar panels. Our carbon footprint shrank before my eyes as I envisioned smaller sinks, toilets and stoves. I conveniently side-stepped the size of the closets.

About this time is when I came across a story of a woman RV'er who stopped to ask directions from a farmer. She noticed a few chickens roaming around loose outside a chicken coop, scratching, strutting and scrambling for grasshoppers. "Your chickens are out!" she exclaimed, "Do you want help catching them?" "Oh, no." The coy farmer smiled. "I let a few wander around outside. The caged ones think they're free, too. They're happier." We didn't know squat about RV life but we were game. Loose chickens it was!

Oscar Wilde wrote, *Society often forgives the criminal; it never forgives the dreamer.* I take my dreams to heart. Not long after that bike ride I dreamt that Jay and I were walking among rows and rows of motorhomes, ooo-ing and ahh-ing as we went. Soon thereafter, Aunt Clara, my devilish Danish Aunt who was never known to travel far from the farm, showed up in dreamtime. She handed me a map and said, "Go."

Aunt Clara, my guardian angel. As a child growing up in rural Iowa I would sneak in my pajamas to her clapboard farmhouse and beg to stay the night. She never refused me. Thus I grew up in her kitchen of fresh-baked bread and wild acres of creek and hills of walnut and maple trees. Now the no-nonsense farm woman who had called me Sunshine was speaking from the grave and ordering me to vamoose! Even Jay, not one to pay attention to such things, got into the act. He dreamt we were living in a white motorhome. White signifies purity, spirit. Indeed, the spirit world perked as I segued between dreams and the valley of Google where I researched our next home.

I spent several hours a day devouring RV how-to books. I surfed the Internet and compiled a list of our ideal RV components. I joined chat rooms and forums and lost my fear of asking stupid questions as I discovered that RV'ers jumped at the chance to help a newbie. The questions were daunting. What brand of MH? (I narrowed it down to three.) How large an engine? Gasoline or diesel? What length? I reckoned long enough to live within but not too long for forest campgrounds. I wanted solid wood cabinets that wouldn't spring open as we rocked down the road. Thermal pane windows to maintain heat in the winter and keep things cool in the hot months. Hefty insulation for noise as well as heat and cold, and day and night shades to soften the sun or envelope us in darkness. It boiled down to a well-constructed space that would ensure my need for silence and darkness, backed up by a reputable company.

Crunch time came when our belongings flowed out the door in the hands of strangers. George Carlin calls it "stuff." "That's all the house is," he said. "A place to keep your stuff while you go out and buy more stuff." What I can tell you is that getting rid of 95% of my possessions felt like a dress rehearsal for death. *Goodbye,* pecan desk, crafted by a good friend. *Adios,* dining room set and six hand-carved chairs. *So long,* my bear and Jay's wolf, sculpted by a pueblo Indian. Farewell to the six-foot-high cat condo purchased from eBay, a trascadero made from Oregon barn wood, and Jay's father's rocking chair. Our decision to take up the motorhome life became real very fast when people showed up and placed dollars in my hand. One moment I was giddy, and the next I went into a short-breathed panic. Ultimately, the empty space felt divine.

One by one I lifted books from the shelf in my study and Jay listed them for sale on the Internet. While Jay's library consisted of hundreds of books that reached back to his college days at Berkeley, mine were more current, like Eduardo Galeano's *Centuries of the Wind* and the latest menopausal tomes. I saved Dickinson and Poe and let go of my collection on Our Lady of Guadalupe, a decision that would come back to haunt me. I secured field guides on mammal tracks and insect lives. Seven bird books made the cut as well as Peattie's splendid work on western trees.

Our rolling home would be around 250 square feet with a small kitchen (*galley* in RV-speak). The more we pared down, the harder it got. My rules of the sacred-keep evolved:

Did I love it?
Did I need it?
Did it have a purpose that wasn't duplicated by something else? (Blender, hand mixer or food processor?)
Would I sell it, lend it or give it away?

I held onto the items that spoke to my soul like the lapis-blue coffee cup and hand-woven shawl, given to me by my best friend Carole. I kept a Guatemalan mask of a jaguar, Mom's old serving platter and the leather strap of antique bells that Dad's dad had draped across the work horses on the farm. Aunt Clara's yellow cookie canister made the cut. Jay was much better about paring down than I. His monastic monk personality barely flinched, even when he faced separation from his Donald Duck comic book collection. He wasn't saying much these days. But then, he wasn't one to share emotions.

No more tethers. That's the only way we'd give authenticity to the decision to go mobile. We could have placed stuff in storage, held on to the house and rented it as a safety net in case our decision didn't work out, but then we would have been looking back over our shoulders at the past. Renters. Repairs. Collections. We decided to unleash all energy into the future and move into the future debt-free. Our die was cast.

I closed my eyes and envisioned a giant braid. My life, three thick strands. There was the past that had delivered me to this point, the present emptying, and the unknown future that was growing disproportionately larger.

Two

A half-hour's drive up a tight, winding road delivered me to a small pull-off where I parked. I had come here often over the years. From the moment I opened the car door I was enveloped in birdsong, a fresh breeze and the expanse of spirit that only mountains can provide. I grabbed my walking stick and began the 45-minute meditative walk up an old logging road to the trunk of a giant, old-growth ponderosa.

She towered into the sky about 75 steps off the trail but because the trail turned slightly away and uphill from her, the casual hiker easily missed her. Under her protective arms, at the base of her grand trunk, was where I went to sit. Pray. Daydream. To tip my water bottle in a toast to the Grand Dame of the forest.

Ever since I was a little girl I've had a special relationship with trees. The one time I ran away I ventured two blocks (it felt like miles at the time) and curled into the fetal position between the protruding roots of a giant oak. Now I joined the spirit of Buddha, who meditated under a tree and sought wisdom. I followed a primeval dictate as I sat in the shadow of ancient civilizations that had protected and worshipped their sacred groves. I came to the ponderosa, she whose bark smelled of cinnamon and vanilla, to ponder. Her roots reached far into the earth and wrapped around mountain rock eons old; her lightning-scarred limbs stretched to the infinite heavens. Grandmother Tree, I called her. She evoked the comfort and protection I had found as a child in the presence of my namesake, Danish Grandma Christina.

Purple aster swayed with the breeze as a nuthatch chirped his call of fall. I lay on the thick bed of needle duff below her shady canopy and closed my eyes as the weight of recent decisions came to bear, rendering me teary and meek. Words squeaked from my throat as I began to tremble.

"Old One, survivor of hellacious wind, wood gatherer's saw and the square teeth of voracious elk. Grandmother, what the *hell* am I doing?" I sat up, as the forest turned still as death. Then, just as suddenly, a breeze arose. The asters swayed again as sunlight broke through a cumulus cloud and illuminated the forest floor. I was in the middle of a tapestry of silk spider threads that spread from plant to plant.

You must write what is given, she answered.

I smiled. She, the queen of understatement. This decision and subsequent upheaval was so distant from the gathering of words.

Then it dawned on me: those webs were there all along, until illuminated. I just hadn't seen them... until I had eyes to see.

Belle nudged my arm, gentled me from my trance-like state. I gathered my water bottle and walking stick, looked up into Grandmother's labyrinth and blew a kiss of silent farewell; but she was not done with me.

Now get down the mountain and find what has been lost.

Ooooooookay, I thought. Were we talking burning bushes here? Weathered tablets of squirrel-etched wisdom? I started down the mountainside, light and unburdened. I rounded a slope and hopped off-trail into an aspen meadow, a different route from usual. A few steps later I was looking down upon something faded red. It took a moment to get it. Two winters ago Belle's doggie pack had slipped from her large black body as she'd chased a scent. This red pack had eluded me on various searches among the green and brown earth floor. Now here it was in front of me: mouse-chewed, weather-beaten spirit fodder.

I believe in signs and omens. They're communications from nature's spirit realm. Nature, from Latin *Natus*, means *to be born*. Becoming. Signs and omens were the props on nature's vast stage of seasonal cycles and rhythms. She gave me the beat; I just had to pick it up. And so I did. I picked up the gnarly pack and carried it down the mountain. I took heart in the message that was as simple as it was profound: take a different route to find what has been lost.

Three

I prepared a fire in the rock-lined pit in the back yard. It was Halloween and my favorite olden celebration of Samhain, the Celtic New Year. This time of year traditionally signaled a time to honor those who have passed over, like Aunt Clara and Grandma Nealson. You only had to visit a Mexican *campesanto*, a cemetery, to witness the rich customs in honor of the dead... their favorite foods and drinks were left on graves; people had conversations as if they were sitting next to them. The spirits were never closer than on this night, when the veil between our living world and theirs was thinnest. Honoring the dead—there couldn't have been a more appropriate time to burn my journals.

It made sense. I had no reason to carry old words into the future. This flesh and blood middle-aged maverick was nothing if not the culmination of my past words and deeds. Paring down to a spiritual clean slate was the necessary intro to any itinerary that lay before me. So it was that I sat by fire's light and flipped the pages on emotional bruises and spiky anger that leapt from the page. I read of days of head-spinning joy, harrowing betrayals and the intrigues of family. I fought emotional exhaustion as I murmured goodbyes to days past and written and, one by one, tossed them into the fire. My stomach clenched as the decorated, beaded books flared, burned neon orange. But eventually the fire died down. A deep sense of freedom enveloped me as I bent toward them in prayer and stirred the remains with a stick. Half-pages of scribbled words, pieces of my life, erupted into cobalt blue.

Death. Ashes.

Whatever awaited me was not to be burdened with old words.

I was *becoming* through the haze of holy smoke.

Four

The Realtor drove up the next morning, parked at the end of the driveway and pierced our front yard with two metal prongs. *For Sale* read the sign. I thought I was ready for this. I wasn't. My stomach rolled over. I screeched and tromped around the yard, threaded my way through the aspen trees and jumped through flower beds. I loved our home named Casa Rosa. I found sanctuary in her gardens and cherished her distant views of the flat-topped distant Pedernal, the mountain that Georgia O'Keefe claimed as her own. Most of all, I relished the rituals I had laid upon her lands. Since my wilderness retreat days at Dancing Raven where I had penned my first book, I had intimately tied my spirit and well-being to the seasonal cycles and rituals of landscape. It remained to be seen whether I could maintain balance in the midst of an itinerant life.

I walked up to the For Sale sign, grasped the cold metal and... pushed it deeper into the dirt. Then I turned toward the house, opened the chili-pepper red front door and got back to work. I methodically snapped pictures of Jay's German beer steins, the zebra skin that he had brought me from Zimbabwe and some vintage clothes. They were eBay bound. We were in the home stretch. Most stuff was gone except what we would carry into our new life. I suppose normal people would have done the opposite: sell the house first and then sell their possessions, just in case.

My modus operandi was different. *Everything* was energy. Every thought and action contributed to cosmic flow that ebbed and flowed. It was right to get the energy rolling and empty out the house before we put it on the market because I had no doubt the house would sell quickly. Signs, omens and dreams had said so.

"How can you do it?" asked my close friend Sandra. "How can you walk away from the things you love?"

I was carefully folding my Zimbabwe zebra skin; I had already handed off the four-foot tall elk antler to a stranger at a yard sale— the antler Jay had discovered in thick Ponderosa forest our first year together. He had carried it back to me for many miles as my body raged with fever. From these exquisitely painful acts I looked into the inquisitor's eyes and said, "Love has nothing to do with it."

I have loved every place I ever lived, just as I have loved every lover who shared my flesh. Love had little to do with whether I stayed.

A few days after those metal prongs pierced dirt we received shocking word that our friend, Ellen Meloy, had died. Jay had recently met her for coffee in Taos where she had given a writing presentation. Like me, she was in her 50s, vital as could be. Ellen, once a cartoonist, was an excruciatingly beautiful writer who rendered the desert southwest like no other. She had just finished a book on the desert bighorn. Her last email to me, however, was full of tiredness; she was looking forward to a break from her pen. Now she was gone, dead at the end of a long teaching day as she lay in bed and talked with her husband. She simply went silent, mid-sentence. Ellen's death was much more than a sign to Jay and me. It was a profound call to live now.

Five

I added a few drops of vanilla to a cup of water and placed it in the hot oven to fill the house with luscious aroma, to ensure a cozy, homey smell to greet the Realtor and his clients when they opened the door. Casa Rosa was spacious, empty and beauty-full as I locked the door and walked away. We were on our way to Denver and our first RV show. We'd done everything possible to coax a sale; we'd even bought a cheesy effigy of St. Joseph, the Patron Saint of House Sales, and buried his plastic likeness upside down at the entrance of the driveway.

A Starbucks breve was just the ticket as we took a breather from the RV throngs. Two sips in, the cell phone rang. Our Realtor in Taos had an offer on the house. We countered. The buyer countered, we accepted. I would later discover a figure I had scribbled months earlier in my journal as I contemplated selling the house. It was my dream amount, exactly what we would need to kick off this new life. It was a number far and away more than the market price and it was the exact price we received.

Closing date was the Ides of March. As if on cue I found a motorhome online that met our qualifications. A 2002 Winnebago Adventurer with only 14,000 miles in like-new condition. The owners in Kentucky responded to my email. We bickered a little over the phone ("God help the person who comes up against you," Jay said) and agreed on a price. They also paid Jay's airfare to the Bluegrass State.

Six

She cast a ghostly presence out the window of Casa Rosa. She was huge! My petite 5'4" frame was dwarfed at her front bumper but when I moved around to her side and stepped up the stairs it was over-the-top-exciting. A rolling home. We invited several friends and christened her *Tortuga*, Spanish for turtle, with a cold bottle of bubbly. She was destined to be our slow-moving home with huge windows to the world.

There was a pull-out hardwood pantry for canned goods and a real porcelain toilet. A queen-sized bed and a writing desk filled the bedroom. At the push of a button the driver's side expanded, widening the kitchen and living room space by three feet. Another slide opened on the opposite side near the back, expanding the bedroom, closet and hallway. It was a mind-boggling, roomy transformation.

I decorated window valances with brightly colored Guatemalan cloth and silky shawls, wearable décor. I cut a purple oil-cloth cover for the booth table and covered the splashy beige flowers on the couch with a latte-colored suede-like cover. Off with the floral bed spread (a hit at the yard sale) and on with a lime-green cotton quilted bedspread topped with a coral silk cover.

We were on auto pilot pointed sunny south, sorting, selling and tossing. Dishes, rattles and drums. Bedding and thousands of photographic slides from my archives. It was the final yard sale boogie: snowshoes, downhill skis and the camera backpack I had purchased for a photo assignment in Zimbabwe. This wasn't just a discard. I was letting go of the props that had defined me.

Then there was the little Singer sewing machine that Mom had given me in 1970 when my daughter Hope was born. I'd made Hope's first dresses on that machine, seamed many a curtain for our tiny apartment. The frail woman who bought it was profoundly thankful. She could never have afforded a new one, she said.

My emotionally shellacked Danish dad was never one to give gifts but when I was in high school he returned from a short trip with a mug for me that turned out to be one heck of a premonition. It read *CHRIS "Travelers" friend*. A short form of St. Christopher, Patron Saint of Travelers, especially of motorists. I kept that.

Seven

It was my final visit to the Grandmother Tree. Four female deer crossed the trail before me, a short distance from her bough. Four, an auspicious number, ancient symbol of balance. The four directions (east, south, west, north); four elements (fire, air, water, earth); four seasons.

I sat cross-legged beneath her branches and the tears began to flow in a giant release of relief. As was her way, Belle lifted from her resting place and lumbered over to nudge my face... to let me know that all was well. I lay down and looked up into the expanse of green as if I could magically memorize the feel of sky and cloud through long slim needles.

I eventually rose, lit a piece of sage and encircled the Queen of the Forest. Four times. For protection. I would no longer be around to watch out for her, to confront the forest-thinning rangers when I heard the roar of their chainsaws.

I untied the ribbon and opened the tattered silk box that contained feathers I had collected over many years. A wing from a road-killed ferruginous hawk I had come upon, having just delivered Hope to college. For over a decade the wing had wafted sage and sweet grass, awakening my senses, settling the soul. Next to the wing was a great horned owl feather I'd found beneath his roosting branch. These signatures of flight rested with a splendid sable plume, fallen from a golden eagle, her life stolen by an electric power line.

I would leave the feathers here. I nestled the owl feather into Grandmother Tree's thick bark. I followed with the eagle plume but when I pushed, it met resistance and stopped short. A close look revealed something shiny inside the bark. I prodded a bit; dug with the hard end of the feather and extracted an inch-long crystal. My mind spun in disbelief.

How was it I had trod into this mountain years ago, found this tree and in a fit of magic serendipity found and dug a crystal from her bark? My mind darted to figure it out as Grandmother Tree intervened.

It doesn't matter, she said.

In other words, *Get out of your head, Christina.* Out of my head and out of the forest. It was time to go. I was done; nothing more to say or beseech, and I've never been good at goodbyes.

Swept clean, she whispered as I turned to walk away.

Yes. My life reduced to a few beauty-full things, a blank who-am-I slate and a motorhome in the driveway.

As was her way, She wasn't through with me. *You cannot chase what is meant to be.*

I approached and leaned my back into her trunk, to absorb the power of She. Then I rolled over, belly to bark, and kissed the Queen of the Woods goodbye.

"No chase,' I promised.

Off you go, she said. *Now grow your hair long!*

I gave Her one last look and softly chuckled through my tears. Spirits and their irrepressible coyote.

Eight

Cupboards closed. Check.
Inside doors secured. Check.
Roof vents down. Check.
Windows closed. Check.
TV antennae down. Check.
Slides in (pick up that bra!). Check.
Hydraulic jacks up. Check.
Door locked and stairs in. Check.
Pooka. Where's Pooka? Ah, behind the couch. Check.
Belle. *On* the couch. Check.

Jay started the engine and backed up slowly, *very* slowly, with the help of the nifty TV screen on the dash showing what's behind. I stood behind, way back at the edge of the road to ensure he didn't go off the edge and into the ditch. Thus began the process of working out hand signs. Sharp right. No, sharper. Pull forward. Stop! Okay, c'mon back. Slowly straighten the wheels. Got it!

Jay steered Tortuga down the road and I followed in the car. We were on our way. Our first destination: one mile to the RV park in Taos. We were virgins after all, with a lot to learn. Correction: *everything* to learn. We pulled in, registered, and I drove the Honda ahead to our assigned spot. I parked sufficiently away and directed Jay into our resting spot for the night. We hooked up to campground electric, water and sewer for the first time. Thirty-amp plugs, drinking water hose (yes, they are different from garden hoses) and the accordion-like black water hoses that carried our gray water and sewage into the central septic system. We barely finished before dark. I was exhausted and so excited I could hardly sleep. The next morning we reversed the process. Unhooked all the hoses turned the key and off we went, Albuquerque-bound. We still had to get the car outfitted with her braces, the metal hardware that would adorn her front and fit securely into the hitch onto the back of Tortuga.

Two days hence, the time had come. I glanced across to Jay as we reached and touched little fingers, a loving gesture that became our ritual with every start of the engine. The Honda securely attached to the rear of Tortuga, we crept onto the road. Nervous. Watchful. I'll never forget that first stop sign and corner: we waited until there was no traffic in sight from either direction to make the wide turn. Tortuga with car: 45 feet!

We finally broke 30 miles an hour as we edged our way through stop lights and double turning lanes; we left black tire marks on only two curbs as we headed south on I-25. Six months from that monumental bike ride, I cast Jay an excited smile and scribbled a sign:

I used to make fun of 'em,
Now I am one of 'em!

Nine

Wrapped in glass, the world seen from the road was never so vast. We drove 55 mph. No need for speed. Life had no timetable. I sighed as tears welled. Oh my god, I'd done it! I'd survived the sorting, separation, burning, tossing, and selling! Who can predict the ways of the soul? I had become the person I had cursed from a distance, encased inside a slow, gas guzzling metal behemoth. Now this very vehicle was carrying me into an exciting unknown. I sank into the plush, high-high-backed seat, propped my feet on the dash and started to read the map, adding road signs to my spiritual repertoire.

Picture this: my new home was 8½ feet wide and 10 feet tall. Tortuga's tanks, situated on her underbelly, held 80 gallons of fresh water. The black water sewage tank held 50 gallons of waste, almost two weeks' worth. The gray tank held 54 gallons of shower and sink water drainage. That meant that we could sit for days in remote places that didn't cost a cent. *This* was freedom.

Tortuga moved down the road like the turtle she was named for, gently rocking back and forth. She gave as she moved. She had to. Without flexibility her bolts would pop. Zen monks teach that in every menial task there is something to be learned and something the student can meditate on later. Every mundane task connected with Tortuga was spiritual fodder. Without flexibility we fall apart, yes. And don't forget to empty the black tank every few days. It's not good to carry old shit around. It's heavy. It weighs down the soul.

We were Arizona-bound. This would give us springtime on the Sonoran desert outside of Tucson and a visit with good friends who lived near Bisbee. It would also give us an opportunity to learn the ways of Tortuga. Or rather, time for her to teach us.

It took roughly 130 miles to put my first RV fantasy to rest. Turn right or turn left, follow whims and explore? Y'gotta be

23

kidding. Ten tires and 45 feet of metal don't turn on a dime and head down just any road. Map reading was a high priority, and I juggled three: a state map of topos that elucidated contours and roads that weren't major highways, a regular road atlas and an RV guidebook.

Our first planned stop was the Bosque del Apache wildlife refuge, wintering ground for tens of thousands of sandhill cranes, snow geese and ducks. I had made a yearly sojourn there for many years and had included it as a sacred site in my second book, *New Mexico's Sanctuaries, Retreats and Sacred Places*. I'd never spent the night near the water's edge.

We unhooked the car and commenced to park. It wasn't pretty, unless you count pretty funny. I'd read that there's an unspoken rule among RV'ers that you don't watch others back into their sites. Best to ignore the mistakes and misjudgments. I hoped that others were abiding as we made several exasperating attempts to pull forward and back. Standing outside, I judged Tortuga's length, width and turning radius. I shuffled back and forth to keep an eye on both sides as well as overhead for sneaky tree limbs that might tear her roof. It was concentration time.

Once she was parked, I pushed the button on the dash and leveled the beast—er, turtle. I pushed more buttons and extended the slides. *Very* cool. Belle needed to pee and Pooka was screeching to go out to check out her new kingdom, leading me around by her leash so people could admire her six pounds of spotted presence. She was living up to her name: Pooka, an Old English word meaning *ghost-like*, an impish or mischievous spirit. At only a year and a half old, her no-fear spirit prevailed. She took to her new halter and learned to walk on a leash. She was a good match for life in a small space. Bengals have a pelt instead of a coat. They feel like satin to the touch, only shed an occasional hair, and have no dander.

Our ritual of arrival complete, we headed up the gravel Bosque road at sundown and climbed an old railroad bed to view a pond splotched with thousands of snow geese. Arm-in-arm, we watched as sandhill cranes drifted long-legged low in search of a night's shallow roost. Their prehistoric cries tugged the brain as geese flapped Rorschach lines across the sunset sky. We stood in wonder as they dove-skid-splashed to a stop amidst a deafening chatter of clucks and quacks. Auditory ties that rose and fell with sun's descent.

Suddenly, all movement ceased. Silence fell at the cusp of darkness. Just as the mind was tricked into thinking the world was asleep, water erupted in a winged curtain from across the mere. A tsunami wave of white moved closer and closer. Feather and beak spread across the sky, a snow goose flap massage in a space full of promise.

Ten

The next morning was my first opportunity to sit for a few hours in calm. I returned to my habitual morning sacrament of freshly ground coffee and candlelight; my communion with the powers that Be: God, Goddess, Spirits Divine. Bird calls at holy first light, the birth of the day. It was a space made sacred by boundaries. No phone, no chatter. No television, no newspaper, not even NPR. Only the wavelengths from the natural world to set me right with the day. Well, occasionally Mozart.

I remembered the day in my cabin at Dancing Raven when I got it. When my pen took flight wrapped in silence… the epiphany that I was creating a space for the unknown to drop into. A protected, dark empty womb of fertile ground into which seeds from deep places took root. There was nothing rational or linear about this. I was immersed in the fullness of time. Then as now, I picked up my pen and began to write.

Perhaps my route will be determined by the women I miss, I scribbled in my journal. *The fissure in the canyon wall where shadow thrives and sunlight touches in golden staccato moments. Possibility trickles toward me like water across a desert floor seeking that place low and flat to sink.*

Jay was in bed, which was good because there wasn't much privacy in this here abode. In every home we'd shared during the last ten years we'd had separate, soundproofed offices on opposite ends of the house. I awoke in writing mode; I preferred not to hear or see anyone in the morning. It didn't matter that they didn't talk and took care not to clatter dishes. The mere existence of another's energy field was a dart to the heart of my muse.

Jay's needs weren't as stringent as mine. A relatively quiet space to write was enough for him to continue his biography of a wilderness pioneer. He claimed the bedroom vanity/desk as his space; I preferred the living room with the big windshield windows. It worked for now.

No appointments to keep. No time limits. No watches on the wrist. We both drove those first few weeks but it turned out that I was the better co-pilot. My eagle eyes were good at spotting things in advance and my attention to detail was imperative for map reading. The stack of books I kept at the ready slowly grew. In addition to maps I repeatedly consulted a guide to campgrounds that described places to stay for under $12/night.

We pulled into a sweet deserted county park south of Socorro, New Mexico, to spend the night. I couldn't figure out where to pay so I knocked on the door of the only other rig, a little fifth-wheel. The door opened and I was smacked by a curtain of smoke. A beer-bellied camp host stepped from his rig, cigarette in hand; the Fox News was blaring in the background. I quickly assessed the situation and figured he was harmless as well as toothless. I handed him our payment and when he found out we were heading south he told us about some hot pots down by Bowie, Arizona.

Unsure what, exactly, we'd find at the hot springs (or even *whether* we'd find the hot springs) we filled our water tank before we departed the campground. We could do without just about anything except water to clean and flush and drink. Then we drove off and left our drinking water hose behind. Casualty numero uno. From that time on I made it my ritual to walk around camp as Jay started the engine. I looked for things unseen, then I spread my arms, hands palm down, and thanked the space for holding us.

Eleven

The smoky camp host didn't disappoint. We soon found ourselves amidst flowering palo verde and mesquite trees, flowing streams, chubby little flycatchers and scarlet tanagers. Hot springs, dunes and desert came alive with the rising sun. It was finally south enough to matter. I shed my fleece for shorts and a halter top as fifty sand hill cranes kettled up, up, in search of the river of air that would carry them north.

This place was a dry-camp which meant no hook-ups. Twas good we filled with water. We ran the generator when we needed power, flicked some switches and switched the fridge, stove and hot water heater over to propane. There were clean public bathrooms and showers. I felt pretty smug. We were living on practically nothing, using a teensy amount of resources.

The place was brimming with fellow gypsies. There were a couple of soakers our age from Maine and a pudgy 70-something couple from Alaska who fifth-wheeled down every winter. A pair of ranchers made their way from a few miles up the road and a few tattooed teens were tent-camped down the road a ways. There we were, blessed and naked as the hot waters flowed over our hodgepodge of body types.

The day's new sun poured through the window above the sink, glancing off the round glass pendulum I had fixed to the frame. I sipped my coffee, awash in rainbows of moving color. All was right with the world. Very right. I tied Pooka—aka Miss Attitude—to a lead and walked Belle down the road along the stream. I was heading back inside to set the flame under my second and final cup of java when a small, dented pickup muscled its way through the sand into the campground. Two (*very*) wide-bodied women rocked away in the bed. The driver's door creaked open and a beanpole-thin man with a long gray beard unfolded from the compact seat. A pudgy 20-something guy in a ragged t-shirt and old jeans exited from the passenger side. This group wasn't here for a luxurious soak. They rummaged around the back of the pickup, pulled out a couple of strange looking gizmos and fanned out from the truck.

Oh Lordy: metal detectors. It was school day for Jethro, who was under the tutelage of Gramps. Off they moved across the sand, two men and two detectors that let loose with blaring dog-toy-like squeaks whenever it sensed treasure in the earth. The women waddled along behind with shovels and sifting screens, a modern day hunting party. I sat back with my coffee to watch my personal episode from *The Beverly Hillbillies*. (Another good thing about tinted windows. People can't see me looking out.)

The handheld search machines went off every few seconds, signaling booty as the women dug and sifted. Turned out the old fella was short-tempered in his teaching style. There were too many false alarms and too much wasted digging. Gray Beard yelled at the young'un to adjust his machine's sensitivity so it wouldn't go off for every beetle in the dirt.

"Crank that thing down!" he angrily repeated. "There's a high-high and there's a low-low," he insisted. Over and over again.

Yes. A high high and a low low. In a world of black and white, my world felt infinitely gray, yet there it fell, right onto my lap: a warning in the practice of extremes. I hadn't asked for a sign, and I wasn't looking for omens. I should have paid more attention.

Twelve

Jay appeared from the bedroom late morning and we commenced fine-tuning the second half of our living space: the space outside the door. With directions in hand we pulled down the awning to create an instant porch. Then we put it up again. And took it down. Put it up. Took it down. We repeated the several-step process until we could do it in our sleep, which according to Murphy's Law was exactly when a storm would blow in.

We unpacked the plastic woven turquoise mat and stretched it from under the stairs to create a portable patio and sand-free space. We set up folding chairs and small tables. A larger table held the grill, which we hooked up to Tortuga's large propane tank. Bikes came off the rack and leaned against Tortuga's side. Darned if we didn't have a fold-up yard to go with our house!

And our work had doubled. Inside *and* outside had to be packed and unpacked with each move down the road. Attention to detail was imperative. A ripped-off vent, an unrolled awning, a disengaged car—one slip of concentration could mean days in a repair shop and big bucks. And so I did what every menopausal woman does in order to function: I made a list. And I laminated it.

Thirteen

The Pagan and the Catholic made their way down the road, far from fresh snows that blanketed New Mexico. The Pagan and the Catholic, me and Jay, in that order. A most unlikely match except he considered me the most catholic (with a small c) person he'd ever met and I respected him as a man who bent his knee to the wild. His life's goal was to facilitate and witness the wolf's return to the Rocky Mountain States.

Catholic, with a small c, means all-inclusive. Jay was a catholic Catholic with a Roman in front. Inherently contradictory. He attended Mass every Sunday with a special devotion to the Virgin Mary, but he was also an Aquarius. He read, risked, wrote and devoured Robert Graves. We shared a passion for "La Guadalupaña," the dark Virgin of Mexico, Goddess Ultimo. He sought sanctuary within four stone walls with a priest at the helm, and my place of solace was in the wild, drum secured between my knees, immersed within the four elements. Birds were *my* salvation, wild lands my sanctuary. I'd never done well with authority figures, papal or otherwise.

Our profound respect for one another bridged our spiritual differences. Jay on his knees, praying before the Virgin Mary, ranked as one of the most beautiful and humbling visions I ever witnessed. Our peculiar spiritual companionship had worked for ten years, buttressed by deep respect for one another's written words. We had both side-stepped the ordinary go-to-work routine (read *no health insurance*) in order to live the writing life. In fact, we were living solitary writing lives on opposite sides of a mountain when we met one another (the subject of *Living on the Spine: A Woman's Life in the Sangre de Cristo Mountains*). Downright mythical.

So it was we entered the motorhome vortex. We'd already broken our personal bests of seven years of relationship continuity.

We'd even gotten married a second time a few years hence in Las Vegas. I didn't see it coming—the Pope crawling into the bed. On Jay's side.

Fourteen

We closed in on Cochise Stronghold in the Dragoon Mountains of Arizona, about to realize our RV dream: to sit in a wild and picturesque place, free of charge, with no hookups. Just us and the land. It's called boondocking, and what makes it different from dry camping like the hot pots we'd just visited is the proximity to others. With boondocking there *are* no others.

We unhooked the car and I drove off on a scouting mission. The road ended several miles into the mountains in a campground that spelled disaster for a rig our size. No way could we have turned around. I backtracked and found a dirt two-track that led to a sweet, level open space amidst red-granite walls that conjured up memories of silly putty. *I found it*, I signaled with a thumbs up and a follow-me wave.

With the addition of the outdoor living space, it took around two hours to set up home. Considering this came on the heels of packing in the morning, driving, finding a place to stop, negotiating unpaved roads and parking, it was, well, exhausting. Would it have been less exhausting if we had RV'd before, as every RV book and chat room had recommended? I doubt it. Right now we were too excited to notice the difference, seduced by the road and the journey to the next unexplored place. We were on a gargantuan learning curve. It would level off. As for now, I needed to figure out how to keep pictures and a knife holder affixed to the wall. Double-sided tape didn't do it. Major bumps were followed by a thump as something hit the floor.

I stepped outside to the strident croak of the Elegant Trogan. Many a time I'd traveled to the Dragoon and Chiricahua Mountains just to glimpse the Elegant in his most northern range. Here he was again. Like an old friend, his emerald green and scarlet filled the sycamore-dotted washes with his mating call.

We donned our hiking boots and embarked on a mountain trail. Famed Chiricahua Apache Chief Cochise had frequented these rugged domed mountains for 15 years, wreaking havoc in the name of revenge for the deaths of his innocent relatives by the cavalry. No doubt in my mind, this place remained his. Every trill of the canyon wren attested to his spiritual domain.

It is said that wily Cochise was never defeated in battle. His son, Taza, took over as chief upon Cochise's natural death in 1874. A few miles up the steep trail we sat and slowly puffed cigars as we gazed over the tangled pinnacles of rock known as Cochise Stronghold. It is believed that Taza was buried among the impregnable mountain rocks. I closed my eyes and leaned into the day's hot breeze. I swore I heard the wild whinny of his horse.

We pulled out of Cochise Stronghold the next morning headed for Bisbee and the border 'burb of Naco. A gas station stop was on the agenda. I scanned distant signs for the cheapest petrol, which hovered around $2.00 a gallon. Then I looked for a station with easy access and high-clearance roofs. Y'can't back up with a Honda hitched behind; we had to be sure we wouldn't get boxed in.

Gassing up Tortuga was a magnet for the curious. First the bald guy asked where we were going. "Heading for Bisbee," I said on this blue-sky day. The next question wasn't far behind: "Where are you from?" I paused. Where *were* we from? I scurried through my mind for an answer. "Right here," I managed, pointing to Tortuga. "We're full-timers. We travel and live right here."

It felt a little awkward. People weren't ready for that response. I was either living their dream life or I suddenly had morphed into trailer trash. On this day bound for Bisbee the man's eyes glazed over with envy. "I hope to do that in the next few years," he said, as his wife tossed him an over-my-dead-body glance.

Gassed up and $140.00 poorer, we headed over to the truck scales to make sure Tortuga wasn't over the limit for safety and that the weight was distributed evenly. After all, she was carrying all of our earthly possessions, from four seasons of clothing to Christmas and Halloween decorations. Counting Belle, we were within a few hundred pounds of the weight limit.

Jay and Tortuga inched through the narrow opening of the chain link fence and into Em and Paul's large yard. It was our tightest squeeze yet with a hand's width to spare on each side. I quickly refined my hand signals and made them larger, then went to work on exasperated facial expressions. Jay's lesson was to trust and follow orders, not easy for Mr. Stubborn. Inches to spare meant *stop!* when I signaled stop. If I signaled to angle left, he had to do it, whether he thought he should or not. Surrender.

This squeeze came at the end of the day. We were road weary and short on patience. Signals got confused. I got pissed that he wasn't turning in the direction I instructed and didn't stop when signaled. I rolled my eyes, he swore, and we both managed to smile when Em and Paul approached with excited hugs and hellos.

Naco was a few miles south of the quaint mining town of Bisbee, on the Arizona/Mexico border. Em and Paul lived at ground zero for the Mexican immigration influx. Once a sweet little border village that straddled La Frontera, it was now a war zone where helicopters, speeding SUVs and sirens ruled the night. There were almost as many Border Patrol agents as citizens. Poor little Naco, divided down the middle by the infamous fence that once served as a runway in the Iraq war. From one war to the next. Apropos.

Em and Paul were intensely involved, setting out water for the thirsty people who crossed the border. They organized volleyball games across the border fence to emphasize solidarity with their Mexican neighbors and had stood religiously every Friday afternoon since 2001 on a street corner in Bisbee as part of the International group Women in Black to protest all war. There we were, ten days into our new life, arrivals with fresh energy who didn't need green cards or water. Well, maybe water.

Fifteen

Em and I had been friends since my school social worker days in Tucson in the late 1970s. In fact, one of our first excursions was a walk over the border into Naco, Mexico, for a fresh fruit frozen bar. Pineapple and mango, yum. That was when the border was porous and Naco was a friendly village of two cultures. How good it was to wrap my arms around Em, smile into the face of a long-time friend.

We pulled up next to Paul's work shed and set up camp. Electricity and water were easy reaches; the sewer would require moving the rig to reach the outlet—a small hassle every 10 days or so.

No sooner did we settle in than my computer died. Crashed like a meteor on the desert floor. Online address book, emails from friends, gone. It felt like a bad joke. Wasn't it enough that I'd left behind friends, my house and most everything I owned? I whined. Then I got pissed at myself for whining.

Patience, Christina... patience.

Paul spent two long weeks downloading new drivers and coaxing my little machine into running order. Bless his heart. All he asked for in return was a batch of oatmeal raisin cookies. Angels come in many forms. Computer fixed, all was right with the world. It was an odd state of affairs for me. My well-being hinged on *that*? Well, yes. My community now lived within that little machine since place no longer anchored me. I was akin to a caterpillar in chrysalis stage, where the innards liquefy, waiting to take the form. What I had no way of knowing was how long this state would last.

Jay and I took in one of the best spring desert flower years ever as the sands sprouted deep purple lupine. We drove the car toward Phoenix and hiked Picacho Peak among mountain cliffs draped in golden California poppies. We birded up Ramsey Canyon where I spied my first Magnificent Hummer. When we tired of birds we took off for Tucson to catch the Colorado Rockies spring training baseball.

But mainly, this new chapter in our lives was about friends. No more grabbing lunch on the fly or phone conversations blitzed with static. It was real time with those we loved. Em and I haunted the thrift stores of Tucson and scurried down the aisles of Trader Joe's, and when that was done we secured tourist cards and made our way southeast to the Mexican ruins of Casas Grandes. It was girlfriend time. We experienced flashbacks from our past excursions into Mexico and Central America when we met in Oaxaca, she on her way to Guatemala, me returning from there. We were back in our element. Fresh lime margaritas and the most luscious chicken molé (mo-lay) I ever had. But then, I always think that about molé.

We lounged within the soft adobe curves of Casas Grandes ruins, slowing in the silence of her spirit-charged air. No doubt in my mind that it served as muse for the intricately designed pottery down the road in Mata Ortiz, an adobe village on powder-dust roads where young and old crafted captivating, finely-painted pots. I admired and coveted; alas, a delicate, expensive pot in a motorhome was not an option.

Mexico, *si!* A semi-trailer truck hung precariously over a cliff and the pot-holed highway demanded speeds of 10 mph as we followed a middle-aged Mexican man in a faded sedan, his intermittent wipers skidding back and forth on a sunny day. Me, as usual, reading the signs. In Mexico, said Emilie, road signs are just a suggestion.

The streets of Naco, Sonora, swelled with adults and teenagers dressed in pants, jackets, and cheap nylon backpacks the color of night. They roamed the pitted roads strewn with candy wrappers until darkness, when they made their run for the border. Under, over or around the fence. If caught by the Border Patrol they were driven back to Mexico and released. Then they tried again. Sometimes it took three or four attempts over several days but most of them eventually made it in a strange Darwinian dance. The United States, in spite of, or because of her barriers, ensured survival of the fittest.

Naco, USA, was a sleepy town by day and a veritable war zone at night as helicopters spotlighted back yards and speeding Border Patrol SUVs accelerated up the streets and alleys. They were the visible, well-paid first line of defense asked to respond to myriad absurdities: the people who risked their lives under searing desert sun for a taste of hope; the frustrated ranchers whose lands were strewn with plastic water jugs, disposable diapers and human feces; farmers who must have pickers for their crops within a small window of time or face rot; and citizens who did not want their communities thrown out of balance by a huge influx of people who didn't speak English.

Jay took to the computer and wrote an article for *Portland Magazine*. I photographed. The metaphors were potent amidst a meeting of human and climatic events: not a drop of rain had fallen for months with fire season on the horizon; the jaguar sojourned into Arizona's mountains from Mexico as our government passed legislation for more border fence that would block his nighttime travels; the average night temperature had increased five degrees while the nearby cottonwood oasis migratory area filled with the symbols of migration: the rare green kingfisher that sojourned from Mexico and thousands of desperate Mexican runners.

One month into our rubber tramp life we'd smacked into a hornet's nest of contradiction.

Sixteen

I wondered when we'd cross the line between vacation and life. We were north of Tucson headed for Catalina State Park, a sweet little campground situated around the mountains from Tucson's city lights at the base of Mt. Lemmon. Thus far we'd crossed state lines and county lines. We were well into our adventure life but there wasn't any way for my mind and spirit to know that we weren't simply on extended vacation. When would the reality sink in? At around three months, I guessed.

I glanced at Jay behind the wheel. He'd taken off his sandals and was driving barefoot. His hairy, muscled calf extended toward the gas pedal. He had the sexiest calves. Pushing 60, he could hike up the steepest of mountains and had a body to show for it. Yum. We neared the entrance to Catalina Park as foothills of saguaro cacti came into view. Em and Paul's Chihuahua Desert, while wondrous in birds, was absent of saguaro. The range of the accordion-skinned giants didn't extend that far southeast. I needed my Sonoran fix.

It turned out all of the spots in the campground with electricity were filled by our 1:00 arrival. Springtime on the desert was high season, and in this first-come, first-served park we were thankful for what we could get. We pulled into a grassy little spot with a killer view of the purple-tinged Catalinas.

Our days were dotted with hikes into the desert alpine and up sandy washes. I relished the call of the desert thrasher, the rattle of the cactus wren and the stark, round saguaro arms that stretched skyward.

Time will seal this reality, I wrote in my journal. *I can be in the landscape of my choice: desert, ocean or mountain. I craft a route and discover my spot. Like a lover's hands I move across the flesh of the earth, coming home.* To *be* home without a fixed home. Beyond the comfort zone of rhythmic ritual tied to place. A familiarity that spoke of when the first night hawks appeared in the sky. Knowledge of the blooms on the Fourth of July. All was well. Until it wasn't.

Until I flicked on the switch and the lights didn't come on.

Within a couple of days we were running the generator for power and we couldn't figure it out. I spent hours devouring every manual. We called an RV place and made an appointment. Now, that might sound simple, but remember, it's our house. We packed up everything and drove 25 miles into Tucson for repair. In the midst of a 100-plus degree day we ended up buying two new deep-cycle batteries. We weren't sure we really needed them. After we'd bought them the mechanic pointed out that there was a switch by the door that had been accidentally tripped that cut the power to the batteries. I was tired... and pissed. I hadn't seen it mentioned in the manuals and furthermore why was the research left to me? Thus, our first RV fight. *"Read this!"* I yelled as I threw the Winnebago owner's manual in Jay's direction. What I left unsaid was, "You're the man; you should *know* this!"

We took showers and salvaged our day with sundowners, a ritual borrowed from our previous travel to Zimbabwe's magic lands... a cocktail at sunset as elephants made their way in long, dusty lines toward muddy water holes; giraffes spread-eagled, bending their necks gracefully to slurp. These were the images of calm that accompanied our evening toast to the day. Cabernet for Jay, gin and tonics with a wedge of fresh lime for me. My body calmed and moved beyond the fret-full day as we sat and watched the sunlight disappear on the Catalina peaks. Jay fired up the grill. Rib eye steaks with a side of apology. Humble pie for dessert.

We prepared for bed as the camp host putted up in her little golf cart and told us a space with power would be available the next day. We decided to move Tortuga in the afternoon. We'd already planned to go our separate ways in the morning, me toward a craggy canyon that suggested puma, and Jay up the saguaro-lined wash heading east toward Mt. Lemmon.

Seventeen

The soft desert was wrapped in quail call as Belle and I made our way up an unmarked trail toward the mouth of a distant, rugged canyon. A green-tailed towhee twittered and scratched under the thick mesquite brush. Red-orange sego lilies catapulted the soul. My gaze darted toward the scarlet flash of the vermilion flycatcher. The faint path was a gradual uphill through saguaro and mesquite bosque. Green glade of thorn and spine, bloom and brown. The wind whistled sublime through cactus, the crotchety mesquite had just begun to leaf. A mourning dove rested atop an eight-armed saguaro, cooing peace from her lofty, white needle bed. Seventy-five years to grow that first arm.

Twenty more steps up a steep hillside and I dropped into a small canyon oasis with pools and falls. I sat and dipped my feet into the cool, not cold, stream. A fat little toad with blotches and bulbous toes hopped into view. He sat on the rock and waited patiently for a nearby fly to land a mite too close. A blistering croak suddenly erupted from up canyon. Then another. I walked in search and determined they could only be coming from trees. I'd been hiking and backpacking for over 30 years and I'd not seen or heard a tree toad until now.

That day alone in my single world, immersed within my individual rhythms, was just what I needed. Jay said the same was true for him. We had never been together which such intensity. Even if we were in different ends of Tortuga it was impossible to feel solitary. Our solution was a second rule of the road: we would spend at least 1/4 of every day separate. But we missed the most obvious metaphor. The presenting problem had been the power supply: stored energy bottoming out.

We mapped a route to visit friends from south to north with the seasons. Then, keeping with my family's habit of phoning me only when someone died, Mom called to say that Inga, our Danish family matriarch, had done just that. We had hoped to return in October when she would have celebrated her 100th birthday. Instead we pointed Tortuga northeast and headed for the Iowa heartland. Flexitarians in training, we turned with the primal of flow, the migration of life and death.

Eighteen

Kierkegaard's wonder stool came to mind as the midlands unfolded before me. From my seat high above the road I gazed upon New Mexico, Texas and Oklahoma. Grain bins popped up on the horizon like mushrooms. Railroad tracks disappeared into an infinite flatness. I wondered what lay ahead as we closed in on Iowa, the fertile lands and ancestral spirits of my childhood home. Gone were Grandma, Aunt Clara and now Inga. The Three Graces.

I wondered from my wonder stool whether Grandma had known of Kierkegaard? They were both born in Denmark. Perhaps his reference to *nonnulla desunt*, something missing, had pushed her up the gangplank of the Hekla, docked in Copenhagen harbor in 1895. A plucky twenty-three year old, she left behind a harsh, rural existence of poverty in Jutland, Denmark, and accompanied her lover, unwed. Did she recall Kierkegaard's chant as she scanned the night sky: "Three cheers for the cresting waves that fling me above the stars?" Or was she sick as a dog and stiff with fear?

It took eighteen days for her to reach Ellis Island. Kirstine B. Aaholm, #164 on the official manifest. Niels C. Nielsen, #163, my father's father. They made their way by train to the rich dirt of Iowa where they dug a sod house into the side of a black-earth hill. They had been born three days apart: she on October 26, 1871; Grandpa Niels on October 23rd. He and I share that birth day; she and I share her name.

Grandma died when I was ten years old, but she left an indelible imprint on my soul. She, her daughter Clara and her confidant Inga, the workhorse farm women in hand-sewn sack dresses, were my divine triage: They Who Took Their Time With Me. Under their beds were metal chamber pots, the alternative to midnight excursions to the outhouse on wintry nights. I would plant my toasty little buns on the cold-rimmed pot, pee and vault back to bed. No matter which cold bedroom in which simple farmhouse, I was drawn against ample breasts that warmed me back to sleep.

Now Inga's death was returning me to their simple homes. Strange how these women who circled my soul lived in one place for all of their lives. Stranger still that I eschewed their lives of permanent place for a life of many homes and places, and now this home on wheels. A rolling home that contained the maroon and gray quilt, hand-sewn from Grandma's winter coat and the *Betty Crocker Cookbook* that Aunt Clara had given me when I left home at seventeen. On the bed were two matching pillow cases crocheted by Inga. In the cupboard over my head as I slept was Grandma's bible and the tattered, tiny suitcase with metal latches that Inga had packed on the day she married.

Always a patient grandmother figure who shuffled across her chilly linoleum floors, Inga instilled the love of words in me when she taught me to play Scrabble as a child. And let me win.

Nineteen

You can always tell a Dane but you can't tell 'em much. Home—the return to tribe where my willful forthrightness was par for the course. Aunts, uncles, cousins... we shared traits oft found alarming and irritating by those not of our ilk.

Tortuga crept into Mom and Dad's humongous and thankfully level driveway. Margaret Lucille and Otto Henry were in their 80s and still lived at home, in a two-story house no less. Fit as fiddles with minds to match, they were testimony to long-lived genetics. The irony wasn't lost on me, someone who had proclaimed that longevity was overrated. I'd never desired a long life. *Every day past forty is a gift,* was my mantra. I had lived as if I meant it, living my dreams.

We attached our 15-amp adaptor and plugged into the side of their house.

Inga and her husband, Sig, had homesteaded on forty acres, carving out a life and raising one son. It was a proud and simple life reminiscent of the lives of their ancestors in Denmark, but with age, it had deteriorated into a shameful loss of independence and a forced move into the local nursing home. Gentle Sig never did make the transition. "I never accepted government aid for anything," he'd say. He believed in a savings account. Sig's anger surged in the throes of Alzheimer's and he took to throwing knives. Inga made the best of what was dealt her. Encased in a drab room with a crazed roommate, she translated letters from Denmark into English for friends, set the tables for lunch and folded daily piles of wash cloths. She was the epitome of grace.

The world quickened with email as Inga and I stuffed our talk into envelopes, delivered to one another's doors. Her spirited notes were a highlight of my life until the day she wrote of a visit to her

49

and Sig's farm. Seems a friend had stopped by and offered a drive, a kind gesture, and innocent, I'm sure. But Inga's farm, by then in the hands of others, had been transformed. The once lively collage of alfalfa and corn, pig pens, shade trees and a little chicken coop had been plowed under into a monoculture expanse of corn. The dilapidated, sloped-roof barn, sweet house and nearby maple tree were gone, torn down.

Inga's large-lettered ballpoint loops of joy shrank with the pain of her story. Then she did something she'd never done before. Two weeks later she sent me another letter recounting the same story. She wrote this one in pencil. As if she had seen her own erasure, my ultimate Zen Master died soon after.

I curved around gravel country roads following instinct and old memory to the prairie cemetery where she and Sig had taken me on magic journeys as a child. Where he had pulled out his old box camera, lay on the ground and photographed the virgin prairie flowers. It was an hour before her funeral. I picked a bouquet of Inga's favorite wild flowers—shooting stars—and continued on to the funeral home. There I approached her casket and placed the fuchsia flowers in her still hands.

When an old one dies, a library burns, wrote my cousin Ole from Denmark.

Twenty

Jay and I reached across Tortuga's console and flicked our little fingers. We were off, headed north from West Liberty, keeping with my father's saying that company was like fish: it started to smell after three days. Harsh, I know, but Dane through and through. He could have said herring.

It had been good to sit with Mom and Dad again. I marveled at their commitment and the tapestry of easy chairs and television that defined their lives in their golden years. Together over 60 years, they had lived a novel. Their daughter Christina, on the other hand, had lived a series of short stories.

I'd completed my bow to my Iowa roots. Mom followed her tradition of accompanying me to the vehicle and a kiss to the cheek goodbye. Dad, frailer with each annual visit, stood in the window and waved, summoning an image that always made me wonder... would this be the last time I would see his aged body framed, his hand in the air?

This simple ritual of goodbye was perhaps the most telling of a people who weren't versed in the language of feelings. All my life Sig and Inga had faithfully followed me outside, stood in place and waved until I was out of sight, their love wafting up the road. It was never more poignant than the last time I saw Sig, who jerked his walker down the nursing home hallway and exited through the fire door into sunshine. The dogged Dane was determined to accompany me to the car. He was still waving when I glanced through tears in the rear view mirror. I should have taken him with me.

The highway lines disappeared below Tortuga as I sank into road reverie. Grandma, gone. Aunt Clara, gone. Sig and now Inga, gone. Their homes merely shells, vastly changed. Their hearths where family had gathered, vanished. It was so ephemeral. If it all came down to naught, then what of my life on the road, my disconnect from a specific place? Perhaps hearth was something we must learn to carry within. There was only a one letter difference between hearth and heart, after all. Belle's cold nose suddenly nudged my arm; as if she had heard my thoughts. She, the essence of heart.

I scratched Belle behind the ears as Jay kept Tortuga on the narrow blacktop highway. Family funerals had a way of washing contemplation ashore on tides of memory. My older sister and little brother had settled contentedly and raised families in the hometown. Despite my connections to the Grant Wood landscape, my soul had catapulted me outta there a few days after high school graduation. I was on a bus for Chicago when I turned seventeen, the infamous summer of '68. Why was it some pushed back and others pushed over, content with the status quo?

According to Dr. Karl Konig, as a third child I'm terribly predictable. (Ha, mom would be glad to know that!) He writes that our rank in the birth order is not an accident. It is destiny. Third-born children are the risk takers who often challenge authority. We form the ranks of those who go it alone: saints, adventurers and soldiers. He forgot to mention rubber tramp.

Twenty-One

Motorhome pilgrims had to be from somewhere and we'd chosen South Dakota as our official residence, where honeybee was the state insect and coyote claimed the mammal spot. South Dakota was a good fit. It had one of the lowest vehicle registration costs in the country, no state income tax, driver's licensing via mail and they were set up to give vagabonds a permanent address. They appreciated our business and accommodated us with warmth and efficiency. So it was that Tortuga and the Honda were adorned with license plates with bright red cursive *South Dakota* splashed across the top: *Great Faces, Great Places*.

We were honing in on that 3-month mark and my imaginary line between vacation and life. Amazing as it might seem, when we began our peripatetic life, global warming wasn't on the public radar. I, on the other hand, was livid that the issue central to human survival was hardly given voice. I questioned whether my travels would lead to a stand on behalf of the planet, a place to let loose with a bellowing wake-up call. "Spirit puts me where I need to be," I'd long insisted, but I was getting impatient.

Then I saw the sign. Wall Drug! Yes, Wall Drug where upwards of 20,000 tourists screech to a halt to gawk on any summer day. Wall Drug, where Ted and Dorothy Hustead began offering free ice water to travelers in the middle of nowhere in 1931. The same Wall Drug that's advertised in the Paris Metro, London Buses and outside the Taj Mahal. Would I find my next great purpose hidden amidst their beaver bobble heads, spurs and jackalopes? Would they cast my soul's calling from a polyester-clad hand in the shelter of the wood-shingled portal? Well, no. But I did walk away with a map of the prairie grasslands. I couldn't think of anywhere I'd rather stop for a few days than under the infinite sky amidst a sea of grass. Especially after the 76,000 square feet of Wall Drug.

While most everyone made the turn for Mt. Rushmore we chose the lonely-empty asphalt heading south, scanning the landscape for our next home site. There were plenty of two-tracks taking off cross country but most all of them had one hell of a dip directly off the road. A fun challenge if you have a Jeep.

Just as the boundary for Pine Ridge Rez came into view (where camping was not allowed), a faint trail veered off to the right with a level entrance. We pulled over and unhooked, and I went exploring with Honda-gal. There was a level spot one-quarter mile away by a pond, out of view of the road. Perfecto. We pulled in and set up camp under the sky's distant rumbling.

Jay boarded his bike and took off down the road as a booming array of thunderheads swelled and strengthened, moving closer across the prairie plain. I was thinking about dinner when the hot air suddenly chilled. One, thump. Two more, clunk, clunk. The fist-sized chunks of ice smacked Tortuga's roof as if tossed by a tormented God. The ground turned white and hail gave way to pounding rain. I hopped outside with a rag to wash the dusty car and just as abruptly the sheets of wet ceased. I stood drenched and exhilarated in clean-crisp air as I wondered where the wet t-shirt judges were when you wanted 'em.

I stripped off my soggy shirt, pulled out my yoga rug and stretched my naked breasts toward the clearing sky. Pooka and Belle looked on as I moved into Downward Facing Dog. Then I felt a little tingle on my leg. I swished it with my hand, lay down and began to stretch my back. Another tingle. Something teensy, crawling. I swiped it, but it stuck. *Tick!*

I jumped up and... well, you know how your body begins to feel covered in bugs once you see a few? I felt creepy ticks all over, then I pulled *four* from my arms and hair. I snatched up the animals and made for the door. Off with my shorts. There was one on the rug! I picked it up and tossed it into the toilet.

Tick attack. Pushed from the earth by the rain? There sure as hell weren't any trees they could drop from. I was peering into my labia with a mirror when in came Jay, dry and cheery as could be. He'd taken shelter in a culvert and had enjoyed a grand ride... and he couldn't stop laughing as he picked five more vermin from my back and butt.

Yeah, strange foreplay. But I was naked and he had to take off his bike pants anyhow. Everything turned to hush in our soft, curved prairie place.

Twenty-Two

The pond turned molten at dawn. It brimmed with horny northern shovelers and gadwalls, the big guys in strut-glide showing off their stuff to the unpaired females that circled the far end of the water.

I, immersed in a prairie prayer. Meadowlark surround-sound. Three pronghorn females grazed in the wake of one possessive buck. A lone greater prairie chicken worked her way up a rocky grass hill as the red-winged blackbird scout staked claim in protruding cattails. I sat with coffee, pen and journal. *This* morning, the only thing that crawled up my flesh was awe.

Jay eventually emerged from Tortuga and we settled on a hike for the day. A Colorado friend had told me of a nearby mountain I must not miss. He, a pilgrim and writer of Nebraska's sand hills, usually kept his hand close to his vest when it came to his favorite haunts. We found his mountain on the map, loaded the car and started up the road.

It was a steep, winding climb that leveled off for miles across a seemingly endless mountain prairie plateau. Wild blooms were profuse. Sparrow and lark song drifted across the air. We stopped several times, turned off the motor and sat, taking in the heavenly scale. A couple of hours later we slowly pulled up to the end of the road, a small turnaround loop amidst large boulders, piñon and juniper trees. We had the place to ourselves. As if on cue we kissed a short goodbye and Jay departed in one direction, I in another. I walked a ways and sat down on a rock overlooking a canyon. Knees bent, I rested my chin and gazed on the distant forever.

Soft movement lured my attention as I looked to the side. Juniper branches swayed to and fro... with color. Cloth bobbles. Tiny red and turquoise prayer bundles dangled from green-feathered limbs against a backdrop of cumulous clouds that pulsed and mushroomed above. Raven's call echoed from white-rose spires. We had landed on sacred Lakota ground... a timeless place of power.

I walked across the narrow mesa past more trees with bobbles, stopped at the edge of a cliff and sat. Across the chasm on the far plateau was movement. I raised my binoculars to spy wild turkeys. A tail-spread tom in rotund strut herded his harem of eight. Even from a distance they were huge. They stepped with a gallant air as they pecked their way from bush to tree, working their way out of sight. Seeing them in the wild, I could understand why Benjamin Franklin thought they, and not the bald eagle, should be the national bird. Suddenly, a hen broke rank and scurried to the edge of the cliff. Where was she going? It was a 100-yard drop. A suicidal plunge.

She reached pinnacle's end as her wings burst forth and she took flight. Flap. Flap. Turkeys can't do this! They fly to roost in trees, they run crazy down gravel roads and through the trees, but they don't go launching themselves across 40-yard chasms. Flap, flap she flew... right toward me!

She swooped in like a paraglider and landed 10 feet away.

I sat dumbfounded as we locked eyes. Then she took two leather-footed steps toward me and stopped.

The moment brimmed with holy tension.

This is what is, she conveyed. *There is only this moment.*

I have no memory of her exit. I reached down and rubbed my stubbled leg as if to reassure myself that my flesh had hung on. I remained seated, staring across that abyss, floating between linear and dream time, as my mind struggled for anchors. I had a distinct and eerie feeling that life had dealt me a new hand. I'd best expect the unexpected.

I stood on wobbly legs and walked as if hung-over in the direction of Jay. I departed the mountain in a silence.

Twenty-Three

Grandmother Tree had ordered me to grow my hair long when it had barely touched my ears. Now it hung below them. If I had to wait until it grew long for clarification, I was in for one hell of a ride. Ticks and turkeys were in the mix with splendorous moments and landscapes as we made our way into the stark beauty of the Nebraska sand hills. We pulled up to a little lake off a secondary road for three days. More importantly, two nights, because it was the nights that served up the long-eared owl who(o) sat statue-still in a nearby tree. Watching. Watching. King of noiseless flight.

First light revealed waters of Canada geese, northern harriers, loons and white pelicans in scarlet-throated mate. I pulled the drum from the storage area under the bed, lit a candle and began a simple beat as the new moon rose with the sun. My body instantly relaxed to the soothing, grounding sound. It was no accident... science had long ago confirmed that drumming produced the same vibration level as the earth.

Carole and I once conducted workshops in which we taught women the wisdom of their cycles. Most women don't know they have different dreams on new and full moon, that we once menstruated in sync on the dark of the moon. Drumming was an integral part of our teachings. Every woman who embarked on this 7-week workshop who wanted to conceive a child, did, regardless of prior infertility problems and loss of hope. Drumbeat is a primal, healing force.

Ovenbirds sang from the shoreline rushes as a great blue heron stood statuesque in shallow waters. I moved a sage stick like a wand over the candle flame and fanned the pungent smoke around my body. Sage to cleanse, to clear the way for... the unknown. I followed with sweet grass, a dreamy, soft aroma. All of this to mark the delicate time of new beginnings as the next moon cycle began, to signal, *I am here, I am ready to receive*. Given the past few days, I would need all the help I could get.

The next day found us enveloped in frigid winds that blew in like a banshee. It was Mother's Day and I, intrepid huntress, set out in search of one spurt of bar on the window of the cell phone so that I could call Hope, ensconced near her grandparents in Iowa. I leaned into gusts and sought the shelter of occasional stunted trees. I learned first-hand how the sand hills were shaped that squally day, but I did not find my way to my offspring's voice.

Most days I cared less about talking on the phone. I rarely made calls just to chat and it was my way to only answer the phone when I wanted to speak to someone. I had never understood people's rush to answer, to allow constant interruption. As if a voice from the outside was more important than the person with me or the voice from within.

Jay and I plopped down on the bed and settled into Patrick O'Brien and Henning Mankell, respectively, to wait out the storm. I savored hunkering down warm and dry amidst nature's fury. It felt like old-comfort, caveman, reptilian-brain kind of stuff, like falling asleep to raindrop's hypnotic pluck upon Tortuga's roof.

The winds died as darkness fell. I opened Tortuga's door to spanking fresh air, made my way outside to oriole's orange flutter and headed for a formidable hill with a view to the west, determined to catch a glimpse of the setting new moon. The slick climb paid off as I scanned the western sky for the sliver of silver that marked the new cycle. *There she be.* I smiled. And just like that, I relaxed. *Trust the question of new birth, Christina, even if you don't know the answer.* It was me, La Luna, and the soft, low hoot of the Long-eared Owl out there on that windswept dune.

Twenty-Four

We made our way down the harried Front Range of Colorado's Rocky Mountains. Once an exhilarating setting where prairie met mountain, its mystique had given way to population explosions and toxic brown clouds of pollution. Jay had been born and raised in Denver and had lived the changes firsthand. Now his feisty mom was in an assisted-living facility a few miles from where he had grown up. Jay had asked permission to dry camp in the parking lot and the facility was happy to oblige. It was endearing to watch her on Jay's arm as he helped his mother up Tortuga's steps. Lila scanned our home in amazement and she gleefully petted Belle and Pooka. At age 88, she was the same age as my father. It was humbling to watch the two oldsters adjust in tandem to life's end. Their minds slowed and their hearing failed, but their spirits rallied in spite of it all.

We continued south after a couple of days, keeping to an itinerary shaped by the special folks in our lives. By now we had met RV'ers who planned their travels around the best barbecue places and major thoroughbred horse races, pristine golf courses and predictably warm weather. We headed to Bluff, Utah. It was time to see Mark, the husband of Ellen, whose death had solidified our launch into this new life. The urgency of June was palpable, as the sun moved farther north and pierced the southwest sand.

We neared the stunning desert canyons of Bluff as Jay glanced at me and in his perfect duck dialect, said, "Oh boy! We're getting close."

I broke out laughing and tried to answer, but I slung more spit than words.

Tortuga managed Mark's soft, sandy lane with panache. We nudged up against a wire fence in the only accessible shade and unfolded near the desert home that Mark and Ellen had built. It was a few bicycle pedals to tiny Bluff and isolated from the highway with serene southern views to the San Juan River where Mark was a seasonal Ranger. It was good to see the burly guy again. To sit together at day's end, sip G & T's and let Mark ramble on about whatever came to mind... mostly Ellen.

The first day of summer dawned with the take-no-prisoners sun. Jay, Mark and I hiked across slick rock and dune in the potent solstice heat. It was Mark's first return to this special place since Ellen's death. We were in search of their favorite ancient Moki steps, but he struggled. He couldn't get his bearings. No surprise. Ellen was a strong rudder.

I pointed out a faint 2-track across the plateau. "Never noticed that before," Mark said, perplexed. I nudged my shoulder into his in a loving cajole. "Perhaps it just appeared," I said, in a nod to magical realism.

The faded trail took us to cliff's edge. Trailing the side of the steep, grainy sandstone were soft foot-wide Moki steps. Straight down. We sat for a bit and stared into desert space. Salty sweat trickled into my eyes. I poured water onto my kerchief and wiped away the burn; tied the wet, cool bandana around my neck. As if on cue Mark rose, turned in silence and ambled back across the plateau, deserting Jay and me to descend the ruddy-red, cliff-side steps of ancients. My little feet learned to trust sandstone that day. To cling like the red-spotted lizard that abruptly appeared next to my grasping hand.

Once down the cliff steps, Jay and I dropped into an intriguing canyon. It brimmed with more ruins, but it was too danged hot to enjoy it or go on side trips. We returned to the house exhausted and drained in 105-degree heat. "I've never done it this time of year," Mark quipped, as if he'd had nothing to do with the excursion. I looked at him with questioning eyes as I remembered his dreamy state up there on the plateau. I wondered whether he wasn't trying to follow Ellen into other realms.

Showered, refreshed and restored, I made my way to Mark's garden. We needed some focus, and Christina was about to hold forth. I picked a half-dozen bushy basil branches. I collected olive oil, nuts and fresh parmesan cheese from Tortuga and headed for Mark's ample kitchen sink where I rinsed the emerald green leaves of the day's dust and packed them into the blender's glass pitcher. It whirred away as I slowly added salt, cheese and olive oil. No mere pine nuts today. I tossed in a macadamia, pecan and cashew combo and topped it all with fresh garlic cloves, still damp from their earthy home.

Pesto divine.

Like our walk through globe mallow and across the sand-shaved slick rock—like the discovery of that faded trail across Ellen's country—it would never be repeated.

Death had hollowed the shell called home. A loved one gone left closets full of clothes. Shoes in a row. A jacket hung by the door. A date book of future plans. A pillow laden with a mate's one stray hair. A fountain pen on the desk, deserted by the hand that forced ink from its nib.

A ghost town of gestures through empty air.

"Would you like me to clear the closet of Ellen's clothes?" I asked Mark.

He barely managed, "No."

Mark and I sat on the flagstone patio at dusk. Space informed and formed by the San Juan River's canyon thrusts that flowed beyond the pasture to the south.

"Do you think there's an afterlife?" I asked. "I mean, is Ellen out there, somewhere?"

Mark sat back in his chair and looked up to the heaving, cumulous sky. "I believe in clouds... only now." A few hours later a micro-wind blasted its way down the canyon, made chaos out of the patio where we had sat, and heaved Tortuga's awning up and over her roof. Ellen had come a'calling in the face of "only now."

Twenty-Five

Good news—our first insurance claim was easy. Bad news—we had to have the work done by a Winnebago dealer. We were heading north, it looked like, to Ogden, Utah. We tied Tortuga's awning to her side and said goodbye to Mark... and Ellen!

There were no awnings at the Ogden Winnebago dealer's. They had to order one and it was the cusp of the Fourth of July weekend. We could wait around Ogden for a week or continue on our way and return in late summer as we looped back through. It was a no brainer. Forests filled with noisy holiday campers were not for me, despite the ear plugs and blindfold I carried everywhere. Get me outta Dodge.

We moseyed north across the Idaho border and stopped along the mighty Snake River in a mosquito-packed park. A couple days later we found ourselves on a gravel back road leading to Little Silver Creek. This non-descript place had it all: a gushing trout stream, rotund rabbit brush and the potent smell of sage. Small, craggy mountains lined the distance; sleek trout lifted and curled from the water. We were gloriously human-alone.

I was back in the butt-bumping kitchen the next morning, boiling eggs and potatoes in a ritual of comfort and taste. I had a craving for Aunt Clara's family-famous potato salad. The secret, she taught me, was to cut the potatoes into small pieces so the dressing would absorb. I peeled the eggs and watched July unfold in lazuli bunting's flight. It was any summer day to the bending grass, the trout that camped in a hole ten feet upstream, the meadow lark that sent his trill across the willow tips. Dragon flies ruled, one with wings that resembled a gold eagle feather, another that looked like a black and white biplane.

These were the kinds of places I'd come to cherish—quiet, out of the way secrets. The lonesome beauty of the all too ordinary.

There was nothing sexy about them. No development. No signs. No spoon-fed entertainment. Humdrum hell to most, and just my cup of tea. The quintessence of motorhome Zen.

Potato salad secured in the fridge, Jay sat by the creek and read *Moby Dick* for the third time as Belle and I took to a serpentine path that followed the creek. A stocky kingbird came and went on his dried mullein perch, as I hop-stepped along the water. Suddenly, boom! A gray partridge and her dozen chicks burst like shooting stars from their hidden grass nest. Plump little wedge-winged flaps, they only carried a couple of feet. Excited, Belle gave chase and caught one in her soft retriever mouth. She turned, so proud, walked the tiny feather mound to me, and dropped it into my hand. Covered with slobber, unhurt, it darted off, zip!

Our 4th of July afternoon found us body surfing our way down Silver Creek's cool, small rapids. It was pure glee until Jay sank into a muddy hole underneath the water that sucked the Keen sandal right off his foot. We poked sticks and dove into murky waters to no avail. The river God had claimed a prize. We retreated to Tortuga and noticed that the refrigerator was off. The inside propane gauge read ½. So did the outside. We had plenty of fuel so what was the problem?

First no awning, now no fridge.

I was bummed. I didn't know how Jay felt. He remained stoic to whatever dilemma. We had hoped to stay at least a week. Now we were forced to pull out after only four days. Jay made his Tortuga-way up the bumpy two-track and back to the main road as I walked the plot and looked it over for anything left behind. No dog leash tied to a tree, no errant trash. And then I put my right hand over my heart and gave a little bow, a thanks to the land for holding us. It's a two-way deal, after all.

We'd no more hit the highway when we met a fresh layer of chip-seal blood pressure elevator. Cars and trucks were whizzing by, ignoring the slow speed limit and the loose rock signs. It was a bona fide asphalt assault. We took three big hits to the windshield. The day could only get better.

A little windshield repair place drilled and filled the chips and directed us around the corner to an RV repair place. The old guy in coveralls was kind enough not to laugh as he told us that all the propane fridge needed was enough electrical charge to start it. We figured a propane fridge ran on, well, propane. Since we'd been boondocking and off electricity, our batteries were down. The little ten-volt solar panel that came with Tortuga was designed to handle only the phantom loads, like the illuminated face of the VCR. A full-sized solar panel made our wish list.

Yeah, right. We could have turned on the generator. The quiet behemoth was built into the side of Tortuga. Thus far we had pressed the switch inside of Tortuga and she'd purred away for the few minutes it took to run the coffee grinder and the vacuum cleaner, but we hadn't left it on for the necessary hour to give the batteries a little charge. That's all it would have taken since we used so little power. It's not like I was watching *The Young and the Restless* every day.

The RV guy was finishing up when we discovered a syrupy red pool in one of our bins. He figured it to be a loose connection in the lubricant line to the slides. He tightened it down and added more.

Did someone say high-highs and low-lows? I half-stomped my way into the Hailey Post Office to pick up our monthly mail from our South Dakota mail service. *Please, God, let there be a* New Yorker... *or four.* I needed some good cartoons and there was no expiration on good writing.

An envelope contained a letter from my cousin Ole in Denmark. He confirmed his plans to meet us at the Phoenix Sky Harbor Airport in September and travel with us for three weeks. Doldrums vanquished, I was ecstatic. This would be our chance to repay Ole's hospitality from our trip to Denmark a couple of years earlier. He was a kick. I couldn't wait to see him again. Surely, I pledged, we'd have the RV kinks ironed out by then.

I threw our laundry into one of those 3-load machines at the local Mat and, laptop in hand, walked down the street to Hailey's coffee shop for some java and free wi-fi. My internal antenna for hot spots grew stronger every week. Then I bought a few pounds of Hailey's *Buckin' Bronco Espresso* beans, checked the laundry and made my way back to the roving home.

Twenty-Six

A serious heat wave enveloped the lower two-thirds of the country as we headed toward friends in Montana and Colorado. The Colorado rendezvous was Carole's mid-August 60th birthday party. Counting Ole's arrival in September, two deadlines had crept into our no-plan life. Not to worry. It was July. We would land at Carole's mountain celebration via Helena and an adventurous, albeit slow, trek across the west.

We landed north of Ketchum in a sweet canyon cleavage in the Sawtooth Forest. Jay and I spent the mornings abiding by our rule, to be alone. Jay kept to the same morning ritual he had followed since his radical 20s: He rose around 6:00 a.m. and had a breakfast of super-nutty granola with plain yogurt which he floated in (are you ready for this?) orange juice. Then he went back to bed for a short sleep, rose for a second time and poured himself a cup of java, whereupon he chose a quiet spot to read his morning devotions. I figured the redundancy was rooted in his catholic nature, like going to mass every Sunday. No matter where his church was, the same Mass was said throughout the world. There was something steadfast and secure in that foundation. I relished spying his silhouette in a folding chair underneath a towering pine, steaming coffee in hand, missal on his lap.

In addition to my usual coffee by candlelight and pen to paper, my mornings evolved into walking meditation and a faithful 15-minute regimen of stretches, working the body, piquing her memory of a youthful woman who moved with ease. A good afternoon was to hang out with a Henning Mankell mystery. And always at least an hour long walk.

Life was good along little Baker Creek as we unfolded into a limitless number of days. I piddled around, lazed and lingered. My new vocation was putter-smith as I capitalized on the years it had taken to get beyond guilt and that pervasive judgment that mine was the easiest and laziest of vocations. Oscar Wilde had it right when he said, "To do nothing at all is the most difficult thing in the world, the most difficult and the most intellectual."

It was day dream and burn daylight for me, open season on linear time. Buddha would be proud, not to mention Inga and Aunt Clara, my big-bosomed Buddhas of the bedroom-slipper shuffle.

Those forest canyon days encompassed a migration from solitary time to joint ventures. Every outing served surprise. A few days in we grabbed our hiking sticks and followed a winding valley stream several miles into a meadow of riotous penstemon—huge lavender, tiny electric blue, fragrant white interspersed with orange, red and lemon-yellow columbine. The word *glory* exploded from my brain as we sat and puffed on a cigar in the still, fragrant beauty of no-time.

A quarter-mile from the trailhead I spied a faint path that appeared to run parallel to the one we were on. Now, the last time I'd wandered off trail I had found Belle's tattered pack in the echo of Grandmother Tree's invocation, *Go and find what has been lost*. It took all of five minutes to come upon a little arch of balanced stones at the side of the trail. It was one foot high and almost as wide, the obvious creation of a Buddha with time on her hands. Delicate Arch had nothing on this perfection. I knelt beside the marvel to catch a closer look, afraid to breathe for fear I would send it toppling. Grandmother Tree, the wild turkey and now this little wonder. It was as if I had entered a parallel reality.

The hamburgers sizzled away on the grill as I cut veggies and tossed them into the lettuce. I had just taken my first bite of burger when Jay said, "I'd like to go to Bellingham… to see Eric." Eric, as in Donald Duck Eric, the skate-boarder particle-physics nephew whom Jay helped to raise and loved dearly. Eric had graduated from Western Washington College in May and had decided on a 2-year stint with the Peace Corps. He would soon depart for Namibia.

My body contracted.

Minutes earlier I'd secretly celebrated our rest-full interlude. In six months we'd traveled a tangled trail across New Mexico, Arizona, Texas, Oklahoma, Missouri, Iowa, South Dakota, Nebraska, Colorado and New Mexico (again), Utah and now Idaho.

Six months of setting up camp and tearing it down, drives and scouts and parking. Bellingham meant we must leave immediately in order to be in Colorado in August. My soul said *sit a spell*. The arch had whispered *practice patience* as my brain envisioned time on my hands. But my mouth blurted, "Sure!"

The speedy rationalization went something like this: We chose this life in order to travel to new lands and see those we loved. We'd just *do it*. No big deal. I'd get my rest… eventually.

Onward I went, frazzle compass askew.

Twenty-Seven

I read aloud from an account of Lewis and Clark's expedition as we followed their route along the shallow Salmon River. Splashing trails of shimmering fish broke calm waters as they migrated up this inland waterway from ocean depths, a miracle movement from salt water to fresh. Upstream they came, to return to the place where they were born and fulfill the destiny to mate.

Wide, wooden boats with upturned ends coated the river, symbols of the desire to hook as electrified men anticipated their catch. Osprey nests of sticks crowned telephone poles as the wide-winged fish eagles vied for their fair share in this ritual of river. I was high upon the wonder stool again, my mind wandering among the picturesque scenes along the road.

We reached the outskirts of the town of Salmon, the heart of Sacajawea's homelands, she who braved unknown lands. The metaphor was not lost on me, who struggled daily across the terra infirma of my body as it shed mother-mode in a cloud of hormonal chaos. Sometimes my body felt like no-(wo)man's land, a collage of shifting gears that ground and clanked. Memory that hid behind corners; night sweats that gave way to vivid dreams. Every middle-aged woman with a womb made the equivalent of a Lewis and Clark expedition.

We passed the sign for Sacajawea's birthplace. A hundred years ago most women were dead by age 50. Now we strutted onto a brand new dance floor in between no-kids and that wizened old woman called Crone. I was 54, into the thick of it. I preferred Creatrix, a female creator.

Twenty-Eight

We pulled into Bellingham and parked in front of Eric's rented house, ran a cord and hooked up to the water spigot. The house was vintage student, with cinderblock bookcase décor. Eric shared it with his girlfriend, a couple of other guys and an illegal puppy. He led us on a walking tour of campus, proudly showing off the spot where he'd gotten busted for skate boarding. We saw his physics lab and hiked up to a major rock outcropping where he showed off his climbing skills. It was the skateboard park, however, that ruled the day: two hours of board antics, dangerous leaps and displays with no pads.

The next morning I took care of the dirty laundry while Jay went to mass. (*Little difference*, I surmised.) Jay never said anything about his time with Eric, but he seemed at peace as we started the engine and pulled away from the curb. It was the first of August. Two neighbors were screaming at one another over their dogs, and an old guy in a golf shirt was scowling disapprovingly at Tortuga from his front yard. I smiled and waved. We had two weeks to make it to Carole's Colorado party.

Twenty-Nine

Jay said the Cascades were as splendorous as the Alps. For the first time Tortuga was seriously challenged as she down shifted until she couldn't downshift any more. We crept-chugged at 40 mph on the inclines, praying for a passing lane, of which there were thankfully many; one driver's middle-finger thrust into the air was enough.

We turned into a campground at the edge of the glacier-cold Skagit River. I didn't realize how road weary I was until my third trip around the campground loop looking for a space. *Just decide, Christina. Park and lie down for awhile.* Jay was beat, too. His face began to take on a look of constant tiredness. Dark circles formed under his eyes.

Twenty minutes of horizontal time worked wonders. I stepped outside of Tortuga and took in the scale of it all. Distant waterfalls trembled down sheer, craggy cliffs. Binoculars were moot. I could hear the birds but could not see them in the thick, spire canopy. I rolled my head back to my shoulders. Peeps and croaks, whistles and warbles showered down from the Douglas Fir tops, but nary a wing was seen.

I hoofed it along the icy river to a Hemlock forest that crawled up the mountainside. A slight trail delivered me to a flat-rock seat amidst dark, lush moss and fern. I, alone in a sanctuary of giant hush. The wind rose. A heaving shush moved through the holy damp. First faint, then slightly louder, the woods filled with the sound of... bassoons? I cupped my ears to catch the mysterious concert of horns. The sound of colossal trunks in motion. I have no clue how long I sat in the hypnotic sway where sunbeams never fell. I remember thinking that if I dallied, however, I too would soon be covered in moss. I had a sudden urge for pancakes.

Those were the moments I lived for, when silence ruled and my tongue ceased to wag. I continued to observe and journal as we traveled forth, destined to witness, to take in energies far greater than my own, to swirl them around my mind and body in wait for some indefinable manifestation.

A few days later in Metalline, Idaho, I pressed the button to retract the bedroom slide and was greeted with a grinding screech and the sound of ripping metal. Metal in Metalline. Over the edge went I. Perking coffee sounded like a hovering helicopter. The presenting problem was Tortuga. Underneath, something bigger pressed.

I lucked out. I unknowingly maneuvered the slide by putting up the jacks which released a fresh stream of hydraulic fluid into the system. Jay, meanwhile, was on the phone to Winnebago trying to get answers. I was sick to my stomach with fret as we headed down the road. Not to worry, said the guys in Ogden. They'd take care of it when we arrived. We were still on for Helena.

Jay and Ben had been buds for thirty years, since serving time in Wyoming with the Nature Conservancy, battling with the likes of Dick Cheney. We headed out to Ben's forest acreage surrounded by old farms and ranches, nudged on all sides by subdivision. A charming white yurt squatted on the property. A simple, quiet time space. A car battery sat on the floor inside the door to power a little stereo. A wide deck opened to tall ponderosa pine. This is where we parked, under the umbrella of nuthatch calls. Where laughter mingled with tender grilled steaks and Ben squeezed oranges for breakfast on the deck between his harried trips to town where he parlayed big ranch real estate deals.

I began to read May Sarton's book, *A Reckoning,* that I'd picked up on a 50-cent table in Metalline Falls, right before the slide began to grind. The book had jumped at me from a long line of tattered covers inside the old depot. I have learned to trust when I am drawn to a book, when it meets me halfway from its place on the shelf.

Thus I turned the pages on a 60-year-old Creatrix. Blindsided by a diagnosis of cancer, she embarked on a meaningful death through rituals that uncannily resembled my recent transition into a roving life. The Creatrix pared down to things that were essential for the soul. She carefully chose only those people to be near who supported and assisted her plan. Her issues were mine—community and home—and she left me with the simple germ of delicate truth: life was nothing if not a preponderance of endings. Every day past forty was not only a gift; the point was to live a good death.

I yoga-stretched into the morning sun as Jay attended to his morning meditation. The distant drone of earthmoving machines crept closer and turned into Ben's dirt lane. They'd arrived to expand a spring and dig a pond adjacent to a building site for Ben's future home. We cajoled the injured slide one more time and hit the road.

Thirty

We slowly turned into the Ogden Winnebago dealership and unhooked the Honda. I was relieved that our awning and slide would be fixed and we'd be whole again. I also fretted over moving out of Tortuga and leaving our home and few worldly possessions in someone else's hands. When the service manager checked our vehicle records on the computer he noticed that the slide had also stopped working in 2003, well before we'd purchased her. Que surprise! No mention in the seller's service records. The miracle was what came next: Chip said, "There's a pattern here, and we're going to do right by you folks." Thus we learned the power of the service rep. He got on the phone with the regional manager. Despite the fact that the warranty had run out and we were not the original owners, Winnebago covered the repair and put us up in a motel as the men worked diligently to get us back on the road.

We departed Ogden with a snazzy green striped awning, an effortless sliding slide, a propane hose that ran directly from the propane tank to our little grill (no more portable propane bottles), and a new DVD/VCR ala Sam's Club. Belle and Jay got haircuts. We changed the car's oil and did the laundry. I paid a visit to my favorite discount department store for a new bra. We maxed out on the mundane and headed into the mountains above Ogden to recuperate.

That night I dreamed I was walking through a forest and came upon a collie dog hanging in a tree, a rope around its neck. *Surely dead*, I thought. Then it suddenly opened an eye. "It's alive!" I ran to get help.

I awoke with a shudder. *What's dying and just what in my life needs resuscitation?* I sat alone with the dream; I'd learned long ago that Jay wasn't available to talk about such things.

Thirty-One

Carole's party camp was near the end of a mountainous road, twenty slow miles off the highway. I scouted a beautiful spot a few miles away from the party scene that offered insulation from the noise and drama of thirty-plus expected revelers. We parked Tortuga and headed down the road to see the birthday girl—er, Creatrix of 60.

Carole and her partner Chris were pounding stakes, securing their little tent town as we pulled up in a bout of squeals and hugs. We walked over a sandy knoll to the stream bank where Carole had dropped eight cases of designer beer to chill in cool waters and damned if it wasn't gone. Ripped off! This was the moment a bull moose with antlers the width of a house chose to appear through the willow thickets; 1200 pounds tromping right toward us, as if that beer had been his. What beer? We hightailed it back to camp and dove into the warm six-pack sitting under the table.

Nature's one heck of a therapist. One time in Yosemite I traipsed across rock into the woods to lick my wounds from an argument with a lover. Sitting still and no doubt mumbling, I was startled by a coyote that appeared out of nowhere about twenty feet away. Just like that my focus shifted and my anger turned to awe. The fight didn't matter. Neither did that missing beer.

Our camp was a mountainside knoll at 10,000 feet where pine gave way to the spatter of willow. Spire peaks lined the horizon; glaciers of snow and ice clung defiant, like barnacles on a ship's bow. I was in seventh heaven at the height of summer's climax, complete with see-my-breath mornings. I wrapped myself in winter pajamas and my long fleece robe. Oh, the glory of lodgepole pine, the teepee pole spirits! Carpets of huckleberry spread up the mountainside. I was home, joined once more with the mighty mountain spirits.

I had a long history in the Rocky Mountain highlands. My 30s were smattered with ascents of 14,000 foot peaks. Colorado had fifty-three and I'd managed to summit about fifteen. I panted and oft-times crawled on all fours as I struggled up loose scree. Those mountains taught the humble lesson of false peaks, as I trudged many hours toward an apex only to find the real zenith was beyond.

Eventually, though, I toiled to the top. Then, awash in crystalline air and an exhilarating panorama of mountaintops, I tore my clothes off and offered my small body to the Mountain Gods... and my friends a photo op. It was the least I could do and it happened in a blink. Mountaintops are frigid and windblown. Rare was the warm, calm crest.

It is said one dreams more vividly at higher altitude. Indeed, the land of thin air was my holy home of dreams. I had felt the best and dreamed the most when I lived at 8700 feet in my little cabin at Dancing Raven. Those years brimmed with special times with Carole, who made pilgrimages from Boulder to the land that stilled the soul and sparked the rowdy. We sat reverent in my medicine wheel and drummed the sun down, made arduous forays to high mountain lakes. We'd crank up "Stop Making Sense" and dance senseless. One night we climbed up on my cabin roof, lay on our backs and watched meteors stream toward the ground. Carole and I, sisters for thirty years. Woman-love.

Carole's plan was for a week up Long Draw. I think the beer theft was an omen, a message that we wouldn't need cold beer to cool off, because the party was deluged by pouring rains and cold nights. Dry firewood was hard to come by and tents were swamped. Her die-hard group met the challenges and muddled through. When the sun broke through, the artist painted, the guitarist sang, the hatchet cut more kindling.

Carole and I managed private hikes into lonesome canyons to catch up in only the way women can. I'll forever marvel at how women cut to the chase in a matter of seconds. "He wants to get married," Carole said. She wasn't sure. She didn't trust that it could last. She was on this mountain to celebrate turning 60 and had recently declared that she was done with men. But I saw vivid love between them. Immense possibility and a broad swath of security wrapped in one another's arms. "Marry him," I said. "You'll handle whatever comes."

More days passed, the group grew smaller and the sun broke through. On one climb above timberline we were privy to hundreds of elk galloping across a distant mountainside. What I remember most, however, was everyone's hurry to cover ground. I wanted to pause, sit by the waterfalls, forsake the scurry. I grew irritated at the rush, but I hadn't extended the metaphor to my RV life, as in non-stop travel hither and yon. As in Creatrix wisdom, "Just because you *can*, should you?"

They came, ghostlike, through the morning mist, step-by-step along the serpentine stream that threaded the glacial vale where brushy willow and struggling aspen led to the cover of pine. Three bull moose, muley heads of thick antler that spread four feet tall and at least that wide. They dipped from tree line into the pewter day and faded away, gangly creatures strong and sullen, under a peregrine falcon's wings.

Then came mother, her morning journey a meditative wonder. She nipped and yanked at willow tips and showed her homely babe the way. Through shin-deep mud and muck, across the swamp they came. Closer and closer, up the mountain thigh to where Tortuga stood. They came and stopped a few feet from my excited heart.

Here I was again, looking into the eyes of a creature that had made her way to me. Mother and little moose had traversed the bogs as if they had wings on their hooves. I could hear them say, *Festina lente*, Christina. *Make haste slowly.*

Thirty-Two

Freedom was what we had sought in this life with wheels, and freedom was what we found. "I want to do this today!"

And I did.

Every morning I opened my eyes, climbed out of bed and chose my path. Jay and I were living our dream. My brown, straight hair now reached to my neck and life was rich. Not in money; we lived close to the bone on the funds from the house sale. We hadn't talked about money, but we were both working on books, betting on the come. This life was about a different kind of richness. We were wealthy in the possibility that rose with every morning sun.

Revitalized from our week in the mountains, we headed toward Sky Harbor Airport in Phoenix to pick up Ole.

We were seven months into our journey when Ole made his beleaguered way through Customs. The itinerary was a large loop around the Colorado Plateau from Phoenix to Phoenix in three weeks. We would travel from Arizona's Sedona and Grand Canyon (north and south rims) into Utah's Zion National Park and Bryce, up the Grand Staircase and across Escalante to Capitol Reef, Goblin Valley, Arches and Moab, topped off with a final stop at Colorado's Mesa Verde National Park. Oh… then back to Phoenix. We'd show Ole the trip of his life, revisit enchanting places I hadn't seen in years. We'd worked out the logistics through email and had agreed he'd have a separate tent in order to ensure some privacy; we'd share Tortuga's bathroom.

Now here he was! Big hugs all around! We were off for the red rock of Sedona and the Coffeepot Café that boasted 101 kinds of omelets. Next stop, the Grand Canyon.

The Grand Canyon—it didn't matter how many times I'd stood on her cusp or the remarkable trips I'd made into her bowels, she turned over the odometer on awe. Ole was star struck as we skipped our way from overlook to overlook toward Yaqui Point. It was Hawk Watch time, the seasonal count of large bird migration. We parked the car and walked the mile to the scenic overlook.

I found the young woman watcher at her assigned place on the edge of the rim as Jay and Ole took off in another direction. She and I scanned the Canyon cliffs for migrating buteos as a sharpie zipped by, nickname for the zippy sharp-shinned hawk. She noted it in her log. The numbers of migrants were way down this year, she said, climate change the suspect. A black hawk soared across the sky. A peregrine falcon swooped into a nearby pine. Numerous raven friends floated the canyon edge. Echoed *kr-aaak!* against her walls.

Then, the distant shadow. A plane, first guess. But no. My spirit leapt with the realization I was watching a California condor. Nine-foot wing span, float of grace. And then another! They floated in tandem, tracing the ridgeline, adrift on invisible currents that swelled and lifted. Gallant birds of the Pleistocene.

I was torn between watching and running after Jay and Ole to point them out. One more skyward glance and I took off. I rounded a group of trees and saw them walking smugly in my direction. I yelled. "Did you—"

"Yes!" they answered. It was orni-gasms all around.

Thirty-Three

The north rim is 1400 feet higher than the south, heavily forested with pine, less developed and, thankfully, less populated. It's long been my favorite. I saw my first painted bunting there. Relying on maps instead of scouting, we pointed Tortuga down miles of curvy, unknown gravel road as I recalled a Thanksgiving hike ten years earlier. Carole, photographer-friend Frank, two others and I had dropped off the rim and backpacked a feet-blistering trail down to the Colorado River. We set up camp as darkness fell. Totally spent and sore as hell, the guys huddled with their packs and pulled out a cooked turkey and all the trimmings.

I had made two sojourns into the Grand. Both times She catapulted me to physical-strain-and-stretch, awe-capturing limits and kicked my butt. Then, in an act befitting a Canyon Goddess, she conjured up a lover to share my little tent. Eros and the wild *are* inseparable. Whether with someone or alone, the body oozes verve, and of course, one is never alone in the wild.

We parked for three days at a dead-end called Jugpoint, a stirring perch a few feet from the depths of the Canyon. The guys couldn't resist a hike inside her walls to pay homage to the Colorado River Goddess. I didn't go. I stayed on top at the edge to hang out with my big black lover dog and rambunctious Bengal cat. This was our longest stop during Ole's three-week stay. We'd pay. Oh yeah.

We shot north into Utah's Zion National Park and camped outside her boundaries at a funky little RV park with a few full-time rusty trailers. Early the next morning we fired up the Honda and headed into the shadow of Zion's massive buttresses, a scale that craned the neck and imprisoned the body in a constant state of puny. We made our way up wooded canyons and laughed ourselves silly as we body surfed down the chilling Virgin River. We topped off our two days with an ascent of formidable Angel Peak. We panted and stepped our way up a long series of steep switchbacks to a narrow cliff bridge, a stunning, scary-to-look-down overlook where Jay and I stopped. Not Ole, however. He headed for the top as Jay and I pulled out a cigar, leaned into the rock and watched.

"Would you like to go ahead of me?" a sprightly young blond asked Ole. "Oh no," he said. "I want your pretty self to be the last thing I see if I fall." And he grabbed the chain for the straight-up finale.

Quintessential Ole. "7-9-13!" he'd spout. "Say the numbers out loud and knock each time you do. It's good luck in Dane." When we visited Denmark he told us that his dream was to retire and travel Denmark in an RV, recording family stories. He was my only cousin to be born and raised in the old country. When the late 1800's migration swept across the Danish lands, Ole's mother was given a choice by her husband. "Go," he said. "But you will not take the boy." Her fate, and Ole's, was sealed.

I poignantly remember the day we stood at his mother Petrine's grave in the neatly manicured cemetery in Horsens, next to the stately Lutheran church. Next to her was Ole's grandmother and the stark reality that he would be buried next to them. That he was the end of the Denmark line. To many, home is where the tombstones are.

Thirty-Four

On we journeyed among the hoodoos of Bryce, winding across Escalante's vast round stone floor, through vivid hawk migrations in the Dixie National Forest and into southeast Utah's Capitol Reef. The trip was starts and stops, unpacks and packs, stunning scenery, cooking, sundowners and an increasingly weary crew. We were halfway through Ole's visit as Jay filled his wine glass to the brim, and more often.

The air was brilliant and fresh at Capitol Reef. Sun dripped light like candle wax, illuminated wavy stone stripes in startling clarity: ochre, chocolate, grass green, banana yellow. I rode my bike through silent, high-spire canyons, rejoiced in autumn's people-sparse shoulder season.

We camped in Fruita, a ghost town oasis of fruit trees and fatted deer. We picked apples from the trees, sat in a circle and peeled and laughed. Later I patted Mom's no-roll pie crust into a pie pan, added the apples and cranked up the oven. Tortuga filled with the aroma of her first pie. Like the lands that enveloped us, it was a sweet-tart intense experience. It was Kierkegaard and apple pie.

Thirty-Five

The wake-up call came at Goblin Valley. I'd first visited twenty years ago when a dirt road led to the mind-blowing rock formations. It was like an acid trip without the acid, a ménage of witches and gnomes in a land of magical passageways. This time the road was paved, there was a new bathroom and little neat camping spaces that nestled against the rock. Our rig was as large as the place could take. We were setting up camp and had just unfolded the lawn chairs when in chugged a diesel semi-like truck. Behind the truck was a 5th wheel at least 40 feet long; and over the truck cab, perched *on top*, was a Hummer. I paused and stared at the glut of conspicuous consumption as it drove around the little campground loop twice looking for a place to park. There wasn't a space large enough. The behemoth had to move on.

Ouch. I looked at Ole whose face was the definition of, "I don't believe I just saw that!" Denmark thrived on small-scale simplicity. Indeed. That thing just didn't fit in sweet little, minimally developed Goblin Valley. Ole shook his head and found a quiet place to set up his tent as we spread out the camp chairs and grill.

We three played and high-stepped it among the land of enchantment, hiking between sheer pinnacles and leaping between cliffs. I was lost in glee as I recalled past trips with teenager Hope, and the sheer fun of hide, seek and jump. We made our way deep into the mazes and got lost. We took our places on a rock ledge as darkness fell, staring into the heart of the goblins, toasting our close call with gin and tonics. What I remember most vividly, however, was Jay pouring gin into Ole's glass. He didn't ask; he just poured. Second round. Third round. I'd put my hand over the top of my glass to signal No. Then he filled his big tumbler to the brim with cabernet. No more wine glass, it was a cab-man drunk. The near-full moon rose above the fairy towers that had almost engulfed us, as chocolate-colored gnomes snuck around in the shadows.

Instead of falling into bed and drifting off to dreamland, Jay and I started sniping at one another. It wasn't so much the words—I don't even remember what they were—as the disrespectful tone of voice. This for two people who had experienced only a handful of arguments in the ten years we'd known one another.

The farthest northern point of our circle route was Arches National Monument near Moab, Utah. We found an RV park in Moab with a little rental cabin, perfect for Ole. We loaded up the car and headed up the mesa top where we hiked across slick rock, onto narrow stone ledges to the base of high and mighty Delicate Arch.

"I don't believe it," said Ole for the umpteenth time. "How can so many extraordinary places be so different and so close?"

I was ecstatic that Ole was so happy. Furthermore, we were just a few days away from the end of the loop when Jay and I would be free again. We sipped port, and cigar smoke rose and curled as the opal-rose, full moon climbed through an unnamed arch.

Then, on our way back to the car, I lost my bearings and fell flat on my face.

It rattled me. My night vision was excellent as long as it didn't get knotted up with flashlight beams, but there were no flashlights on this moonlit night. The last time I had fallen flat was in Denmark when I went in search of Grandma's identity. Fate had brought me to the final day of a three-week trip. I woke up on summer's solstice in Copenhagen and decided at that moment that I would go to the archives and give it a shot, despite Ole's belief that I didn't have a prayer with only a few hours to search. People spent months doing what I was about to do.

Walking quickly with Jay on the way to the archives I had stumbled, flew a few feet in the air and fell flat. Jay and friendly passersby stopped and helped me sit up. "Tiramisu," said Jay, as I caught my breath. "Throw me down.'" He explained that when the son of the earth goddess fought Hercules he provoked the mighty one with taunts of "Tiramisu," because every time Hercules threw him down he drew power from his Mother, the earth. It was a *good* sign, Jay said. So good, in fact, that I found my grandmother that day. In one of the most exciting moments of my life I discovered

Kirstine Berteline Aaholm, born to unmarried Andrea Christiansen when she was eighteen years old. The father's name was Bertel. Aaholm was the name of the Danish village where she was born.

So there I was, back at camp, wondering why fate would have me doing face plants in the desert. Hamburgers sizzled on the grill as Ole told the story of his great uncle in Denmark who had been sleeping in his farmhouse next to his wife when a violent storm moved in. Thunder bellowed. Sheets of rain poured through the open window. His uncle rose to shut the window and a bolt of lightning shot from the sky and struck him. His charred body fell back onto the bed, next to his wife. She departed the rational world that night, never to return.

The dead collie dream edged back into my consciousness as I felt the weight of three weeks of hyper-stimulation. Or was it 8 months? I was like that collie, at the end of my rope. The glorious moments of travel and the subsequent fatigue joined at the hip; bore down on me within Tortuga's magnifying walls. Whereas one could more easily overlook differences in a larger space, it was impossible now.

Jay's rugged face was tired and wrinkled. We rarely joked without one of us taking it personally. The witty, duck-talking Jay had disappeared as we both grew short tempered. For my part, I'd morphed into a little trip-Nazi. Get up. Pack. Hit the road. Hurry, scurry and flurry. The timetables and stops, routes and turns had fallen to me, and to make matters worse it wasn't even working. Despite my relentless push we'd be hard pressed to make it back to Phoenix for Ole's plane departure.

I should have taken a look at Belle, calm presence at my side. With four days to go we made an adjustment and Ole changed his departure flight to Durango, Colorado, an easy drive from our final stop, Mesa Verde National Park in southwest Colorado. Too little too late.

Thirty-Six

Autumn climaxed at Mesa Verde. This cyclical time of descent and decay was my most beloved time of the year. Sun's movement south signaled the end of another raucous cycle of birth, fecundity and harvest. Now bugs and furred ones burrowed under and down. Warblers left their streamside willows and departed toward Mexico's winter warmth. I had never felt more alive than on autumn's golden cusp. I switched the oil cloth on the table to rich purple to match the final asters in the fields.

Jay, Ole and I hiked down cliffs and stairs into Cliff Palace and Balcony House. I was struck by the Ranger's stories of the ancient vanishing people whose spirits now frequented these ledges. As I stood in the massive sandstone dwelling I felt the eerie panic of people under siege; the dire struggle of those who depleted their wood and water and fell victim to neighboring Indian attacks and drought. It mattered little what exquisite structures and systems they developed. Like the Mayan civilizations before them, they had overextended their society: too many people, too few resources. These ancient people prayed, danced, sang and ate... eventually their own.

Ole leaves in two days, I wrote in my journal. *We will soon be on our own.* For the first time since we began this life we had no future obligations. We would head high into the La Plata Mountains thirty miles to the north and sit in the swelling autumn color of the aspens.

This is when I received word from my daughter Hope that my niece was dying. The official word was liver failure; the reality was years of alcohol abuse, cigarettes and gagging herself to vomit so she could be movie-star thin. Lindsey was thirty-five. Two years earlier I had warned that on her present path she would most likely live for only two years. I had attempted to fly to Iowa that Christmas to hopefully connect her and the family with the appropriate professionals and force my niece into treatment. I had developed the Employee Assistance Program years earlier for Rockwell International. I *knew* addiction and intervention. I hadn't stated my intentions; perhaps the family sensed it. Whatever the forces at work, no one was willing to drive fifty miles to the Iowa airport to pick me up on Christmas Eve. I was the outsider. It was their show.

It wasn't one particular thing that sparked the fall of emotional dominoes: Mesa Verde's edgy energy, Lindsey's dying, or pure exhaustion. Jay, Ole and I were sitting around a campfire a few miles from the cliff ruins, swilling drinks and more drinks. When Jay and I made our way inside we burst into argument and the words were out of my mouth before I knew it: "I will *not* grow old with a mean drunk!"

Jay grabbed Ole's suitcases from the back of the car, dumped them on the ground and drove off with nary a toothbrush. And he didn't come back. Not that day or that night. Poor Ole was smack in the awkward middle. I called a friend in nearby Cortez and arranged a ride for Ole to the Durango airport the next morning. The night before his departure there was no celebration, no storytelling. I was in shock—embarrassed and sick to my stomach. We didn't share the thick tenderloins I'd set aside or the Cuban cigars I'd stashed away. I put every ounce of energy I had into holding it together until Ole departed. It was a major piece of hell.

Once Ole was gone, I sat in the Mesa Verde campground and let'er rip: sobs, pillow screams and pounding into the bed. My niece was dying, I didn't know whether Jay was dead or alive, and I had to hike 45 minutes up a narrow, steep mountain trail to get dodgy cell phone coverage.

Putrid fumes, I wrote. *The crash and burn of hope.*

What a strange time of concentrated energy as the world hurled into disarray. Hurricane Rita, on the heels of Katrina, entered the Gulf of Mexico and turned into monster number two. And it was equinox. While it's popularly celebrated as a time of equal day and night, it is also a time of chaotic energy that plays havoc with bodily forces, hormones and internal electrical charges. It began to rain as wild turkeys appeared outside Tortuga. Turkeys! Old friends coming to call, to remind me to *expect the unexpected.*

There is nothing like pain with a dash of rage to cut through illusion. Jay's disappearance catapulted me into the journal pages as I hungrily reviewed the recent months. I figured that although I had no control of his actions, I could move resolutely into what I *could* influence: myself. It was time to dump the black tank, mine as well as Tortuga's. I went outside and hooked up the hoses. Usually Jay's job, it was up to *me* to eliminate!

My mind chattered with mistakes. What had we done to ourselves with our schedule of little rest? Where was my space to replenish my spirit? And alcohol. I knew better. It was a powerful depressant and the last thing either of us needed. Instead of Jay's usual three drinks a night he was up to four or more brim-filled tumblers.

Three days passed and Jay didn't show up. I pinballed between utterances like, "Fuck you and the 'cab' you rode in on," and dread that he was hurt or dead at the bottom of some canyon. I freaked. Belle stuck to my side, licked my hand to comfort. Pooka perched upon my drum on the lower corner of the bed and stared at me with her huge, green eyes. It was time to call friends for help. No easy task for me, who doesn't share my down times even though I'm the first to castigate friends for not reaching out. "Give your friends the chance to help you," I'd say. "It is an honor."

Indeed. Carole, in Boulder, responded with "Hold tight. I'll be down as soon as I can get there." This, even though she and Chris had a family event scheduled on their end. Her forthright, unconditional response overwhelmed me. One friend said to call the authorities right away, while another suggested I wait another 24 hours. "Involving the police is just another complication," said Ben in Montana, one of Jay's oldest friends. "Leaving is a guy thing. We men have to get away sometimes."

Really? Getting away was one thing, but abandonment was just cruel!

Four days after Jay's disappearance I called the Park Service, who called the Cortez police. They began a search for our car as Carole sped south.

That afternoon when I climbed the mountain to check my calls there was a voice mail from Jay. It read like a telegraph: *I'm okay.* (stop) *I'm at Point Reyes.* (stop) *I hope you're okay.* (stop) *I love you.* (stop) *I need to talk to you.* (stop) *I'll call tonight at 8:00 your time.*

I collapsed into tears and relief. Then I got mad. Four days with no word. *He's where? Point Reyes, California? On the ocean? What the fuck?* Tortuga's secure walls suddenly felt like a prison. I seethed as I considered abandoning Tortuga and moving out. Selling our dream life and leaving him to an empty shell. I resolved to never, ever be stuck again. That night's phone call would be the phone call of his life. I had little hope for our future together. I'd left past relationships for reasons less than this.

The phone rang right at 8:00 p.m.. On the mountain, in new-moon darkness, I gathered silence around me and heard him out. My ass on the rock, ever present.

"I'm sorry," he began. "I had to deal with demons." There was a long pause. "I've stopped drinking. I did not like myself."

Silence.

He said that when he threw Ole's suitcase to the ground he didn't have a plan but he eventually headed to the Glen Canyon Dam his father had engineered. He needed to be with his father's spirit, who had died when Jay was 21.

From there he drove to Berkeley, his alma mater, to visit his mentor from his doctoral student days in the chaotic 1960s. Then he traveled on to Point Reyes, the place in the world that ranked as his most beloved, where he had frequently visited as a graduate student to clear his head. *A phone call to let me know you're okay. Your disappearance was malicious.*

"You're a good woman, Christina. I'm sorry."

I perched under the moon in tears as I gave his words and silent pauses my ultimate attention.

He said, "I'd rather be dead than be without you."

Let those words in, Christina. I took a deep breath.

"We're partners," he said. "What do you need? I can come home tomorrow."

Darkness enveloped me as I sat on that mountaintop. A darkness that spoke at once to death and rebirth. No matter what happened to 'us,' I was a different woman. He was a different man. How *would* it feel to see him again?

"No," I said with calm. "You're there now. Stay with the ocean. Come home when you're really ready."

"But the birds in the bushes are nothing without you," he replied.

Thirty-Seven

I made my numb way down the mountain, drained and exhausted. Crossroads do that. That night I dreamed of me and my older sister, mother of Lindsey. Although distant in real time, I wrapped her in my arms and comforted her in dreamtime. This was as close I would come to Iowa and the funeral. I would send prayers and light a candle across the miles, but I didn't trust myself to show up. I was too mad at what denial had wrought and what I might say.

Love is measured by who shows up. It took eight hours for Carole to arrive. When her familiar Subaru pulled in, I told her that Jay had surfaced. Like me, she was relieved he was safe and seething mad. I was a jumble of nerves, and she was the devoted sounding board I desperately needed. But first, the basics. I hadn't eaten a meal in days so she off-loaded her groceries and began to cook. We nibbled chocolate as we walked and talked through the intricate weaving of events that had blanketed my soul.

Should I stay? Where was the old Christina that wouldn't put up with crap like this? It wasn't that simple. There was something much deeper at work and I was determined to name it. Giving voice to the question helped. And whereas the supportive presence of a girlfriend could easily have catapulted me into dramatic action, like leaving, it didn't.

Carole departed, and Jay returned. It was akin to greeting a stranger. In a change of habit I didn't press our way into the issues. As we packed up without a word, I periodically caught a look into his blue eyes, but that's as far as I went toward intimacy. We kept to our original intentions and headed for the La Plata Mountains.

Thirty-Eight

Up, up we climbed, in a state of quiet surrender. There were camp possibilities along the way but they didn't offer views. My soul screamed for sky, peaks and vista. Expanse where my body could open up, turn inside out if need be. We found the only pullout that fit the bill at over 10,000 feet, where we parked in the shadow of Mt. Hesperus, Navajo sacred mountain of the west wind. West, the revered direction of autumn.

Hesperus was, to the first peoples of those lands, Black Mountain, *Debe' ntsa*. One of four cardinal mountains of the earth. The Navajo believed she was created by the first man and woman with dirt they brought from the lower world. This peak was originally fastened to the earth by a rainbow, covered in darkness and decorated with black obsidian.

We eased into the mountain, tenuous, battle-fatigued lovers. Changed, estranged partners who had gone to the end of the road and now were considering a new one. Together or apart was the question as the aspen ripened in patches, deep gold here against pale green there. Much like a woman's hair, that patch of gray that appears beside her youthful brown, usually above the ear.

Nature took over as healer. My feathered friends, a flock of wild turkeys, appeared out of the woods as if to console. For seven days Belle and I walked the deer trails of the mountain thigh through great lakes of sun-yellow aspen. A birthing room of cleanse. Seven, long associated with magical forces and activation of the imagination. It felt good and right to frame this time within the context of that number. There were the seven chakras that symbolized the principal energy knots in our bodies. It was a defiant black and red seven I had seen painted across buildings, signs and streets in Nicaragua during the Sandinista revolution. There were even seven spots on a little ladybug that climbed her way across the tawny grass. And in a spectacle of constancy, every year the autumn night sky returned my beloved Pleiades, the seven sisters who traveled the Milky Way.

Mt. Hesperus served up seven days of sun, snow and rain. Lightning bolts and bellowing thunder. Elk bugles carried the call to mate. Coyote cracked open the night with howl. Owls clucked, as Herperus riled the soul. On the eve of Lindsey's funeral I dreamed she was sneaking around when she was supposed to be in bed. She pulled out her 6-inch long warm red esophagus as if showing off, with a no-big-deal attitude.

Pure and simple, I didn't know what to do. I convinced myself that I had crossed some ghostly bridge between romantic and marital love. Truth was, I let inertia rule the day. Nothing less than Jay's cessation of alcohol would have saved the marriage. Nothing less than the one apology he had uttered since we had been together in over ten years.

Jay took my hand. "I want to take you to Point Reyes for your birthday."

On the seventh day we prepared Tortuga for departure.

And on the seventh day God ended his work… and he rested on the seventh day. What, I wondered, did Creatrix do on the seventh day?

The Hebrew seven, from the root word *sheh-bah*, meant completion, or full.

On the seventh day I settled for false forgiveness.

Part II

Birds of Pray

Thirty-Nine

We gradually threaded our way along historic Highway 50, a desolate ribbon of Nevada asphalt sprinkled with the occasional town. Mostly, there was nothing but sky; empty space to heal the prior days and feel our way forward. We were headed for a dot on the map called Spencer Hot Springs that looked to be about twenty minutes off the main road. Boondock heaven, I hoped.

Steamy pools dotted the desert hillsides overlooking a vast, lonely valley. Distant mountain peaks were frosted with the autumn's first snow. It bore a strong resemblance to my favorite Valley View Hot Springs in the San Luis Valley of Colorado, except Spencer served up braying wild burros. We dropped into bliss ninny mode: soaked for three days and took long bike rides up old mining roads through the chirps of horned larks across the sage.

My time, as usual, was dawn, when I left Jay, Belle and Pooka to sleepy dreams, wrapped my body in a towel and pushed my way up the hill to the grassy edge of a pool. Sometimes I had daybreak to myself, sometimes not. One morning I even followed a rare fit of chatter and began to talk to a guy in the pool. "You live and travel in your RV? That's my dream," he said. He looked to be in is 40's. He was a forest ranger stationed farther south who came to the hot pools on his days off, shedding the uniform and daily shave. I told him it hadn't been my dream—the idea had come on impulse. Out of the blue. We agreed amidst the steam that out of the blue was a magic place. The more we talked the more my spirits lifted above the past couple of weeks. Hearing myself speak of my gypsy life out loud was its own kind of therapy.

Another couple joined us. They were full-timers too, in a converted van hooked up to solar. They were from Philadelphia and had decided to take to the road when they both came down with a debilitating tick disease called Lyme. They figured they'd just as soon live on the road as in a house. I was with my ilk again—people on the edge who considered life from a different slant. All of us dancing the Loose Chicken Rag.

Dream fulfilled, 7 miles! proclaimed the billboard in California advertising a suburban subdivision.

I pointed it out to Jay, then said, "Dream lived, right here and now!"

The farther we sojourned toward the coast the more the pace picked up. The headline in the Marin newspaper said it best: *Drive 55: Conserve Fuel, Get Flipped Off.* Jay did good steering Tortuga along the freeway speedways of Porches, Corvettes and big shiny pickups as traffic morphed into traffuck. We didn't see any middle fingers, but the Interstate felt like some bizarre concrete vortex that whirled us along. We missed our exit and had to turn around and try again. We closed out the day on the slow-going winding road into Olema, the RV Park closest to Point Reyes.

The morning dawned luxuriously damp as Jay turned the car toward his beloved Point Reyes. This is where he had come when his dissertation got bogged down and when his conscientious-objector work with Viet Nam quadriplegics was too much to bear. It was where he had fled when he thought he heard the word *divorce* on my lips.

The reason was palpable. Endless ocean with the tension of the San Andreas fault as cliff and waterfall met at the sandy beach. We climbed a ridge and walked high above the Pacific under a hefty coyote's watch. Damp eucalyptus and Douglas Fir forests made Jay's hair curly again.

We got drunk on the ocean, moon-swelled mass that impelled us to drop our clothes and lay our butts on the sand. I was stretching at the water line when I spied a scruffy orange starfish clutching a tide pool rock. Its five rays plastered tight, the little carnivore waited patiently for her diet of shellfish and barnacles. Tenacious, she was. And patient. Jay said, "If a part of her breaks off, she'll grow a whole new starfish." She was a Bat Star, come to teach regeneration.

Jay and I returned to one another on the mist-fingered cliffs of Point Reyes. Perhaps it was the misty ten mile hike. It could have been the pot of red chili stew I cooked up or the jolt of sea lion barks that sprang from the sea. No matter… the smell of me returned upon his lips.

Forty

I drove up Vision Mountain toward a picnic evening that promised full-moon bagpipes. Sponsored by a local environmental group, it offered the opportunity to sit on the top of the mountain that loaned its name to the largest fire to spread across Point Reyes in modern times—the Vision Fire that had burned the unique Bishop pine. The road wound up and up for several miles in narrow, hairpin turns. Jay had chosen to ride his bike, an impressive workout.

Once parked, I threaded my way through damp vine and bush. A tunnel of dense brush opened to a mountaintop clearing and ecstatic views. Sunset mist over the tip of Point Reyes, rolling hills that led to her lighthouse like so many satin ribbons. The faraway Farallon Islands rose mystic from the sea as the sun lowered himself upon the water like a careful lover. I turned from west to east to catch sun's dying hues on Mt. Diablo. In a show of balance, there she peeked over softened hills, October's full hunter's moon.

I absorbed the haunting bagpipe drone; deep bass that grabbed the tawny slopes. Jigs forced my legs to high-step hop as people on blankets slurped wine, ate sliced wedges of cheese and crunched their favorite seedy cracker. Jay hadn't arrived yet; I missed his arm around my waist, and it was good to realize that I did.

The next day we rode bikes a few miles into the town of Point Reyes Station to pick up a Sunday New York Times and pay a visit to the Bovine Bakery. "Espresso free zone," they boldly declared... "our regular coffee is plenty strong." It also steamed up some serendipity. Time and no customers allowed a quick a conversation with the Creatrix behind the counter. Turned out my *New Mexico's Sacred Sites* book was on her bookshelf at home.

"Got a second?" she asked.

"Sure do," I answered.

She bowed her head and recounted how she had saved for years for a trip to Scotland with her lover. Finally last year they departed on their trip of a lifetime. They reached the shores of Scotland, whereupon he took a breath and fell to the ground. He died on the shores he had longed to see.

"You never know," she said through tears. "I struggle now to pay off that trip but… well, I've never had one regret."

In the midst and mist of the ephemeral, Jay and I drove to an overlook over Tomales Bay. We sat in silence, relished our chewy, flakey croissants and sipped the hot, strong coffee.

I couldn't find my binoculars, a serious predicament for a birder. Then I realized that I hadn't seen them for two days. That was one thing about living in Tortuga; there weren't many places to look when something was lost. Belle and I continued to Abbott's Lagoon without them for a walk amidst ducks, gulls and pelicans, but no up-close looks. It was a broad-spectrum day.

I was on my way back to camp when I made the split-second decision to turn away from camp and head up Vision Mountain to look for the binocs. I almost overshot the fogged-in parking lot and started to question my burst of spontaneity. Fog, rain, many days hence, *Ridiculous effort*, I muttered as Belle and I entered the tunnel of trees. I was set to emerge onto the mountain clearing where the bagpiper had played when my intuition said *No, you've gone too far.*

I turned back into the tunnel and remembered I had ducked into the bushes and stopped to pee on the way down. It was a fast pit stop since people were close behind. And it was dark. The cloud-soaked bushes all looked the same as I felt my way down the mountain. Without thinking, I dipped into a teensy clearing to the side of the trail. I moved in, crouched and voila!—there were my little black binocs, hanging squat-level on a branch. Two days in the damp drip of fog. My far-away vision returned on Vision Mountain.

Fog was the metaphor in this place by the sea. Fog, the gift of damp. The juxtaposition of wild forever-sea and vision impaired. Fog forced one to look inward, to stop in vast quiet and hear the world drip. Fog-white feathers blanketed bays. Fog snaked up riverbeds. Fog dripped from colossal redwoods that made caves of sun-strewn paths.

Clouds came to earth, soft enclosures, trapping sound. Everything that moved was heard for miles. Sandpiper sweet.

Forty-One

Beaches beckoned every few miles as we made our way north. Every sand-laden stretch was a shell-strewn treat, a place of auditory awe. Heckling gull. Barking seal. The thunder crash of waves. Distant foghorn, the heartbeat of the bay—a rhythm so engrained that I imagined a sudden mass collapse of life if that horn should suddenly cease. A harbor seal bobbed the fish-filled surf, hope on the ends of her whiskers.

It was crab season on Bodega Bay where we bought the beautiful creatures right off the boat and squeamishly dropped them into our boiling pot. The Occidental farmer's market offered up glossy eggplant, zinnias and pumpkins. I stepped into a Guerneville salon for my first hair cut since I'd left my gay hairdresser behind in Taos. Fate put me in the hands of Amber, who cranked up the Christian tunes and sang along to Jesus as she snipped the ends off my hair. (*Just* the ends… it was below my cheeks by now.)

My birthday fell on the banks of the Russian River. Six birthday cards from friends and a letter from Ole in Denmark hung by clear tape from the kitchen cabinet. We celebrated with a fresh salmon fish and chip dinner and champagne as otters splashed at river's edge. Joan, a lone-woman RV'er camped farther down on the river, joined us for my homemade birthday cake. She, a delightful 70, said she preferred her RV to the walls of her house.

Women traveling solo were everywhere. I met them drinking margaritas in seaside bars, in the occasional RV park and on wildflower hikes in craggy desert mountains. Sometimes they had pets, sometimes not. My pushing-70 friend Sandra took off for months at a time, leaving her husband behind. But most of the road-happy women had no mates, courageous Creatrixes who didn't put life on hold—*always* fascinating.

That night I told Jay that should he die first I was going to downsize the rig and keep rolling down the road. Ole's letter had included the suggestion that I might want to get myself a little "woman-wagon."

We headed inland beyond dripping redwoods and beaches dimpled with footprints. A few hours east dropped us in the Napa Valley among mountainsides of golden vineyards that rolled and curved with the contours of the land. Grape autumn. We dipped our bodies into Calistoga's steaming tubs of mud, sampled wines and gorged on crab cakes, garlic mushrooms and Greek dolmades. It was deliciously wondrous, but my body didn't open up like it had by the sea. Until I set foot upon Jack London's lands.

I hadn't known his home was near. His book of short stories was one of the few books I carried with me. Ever since we'd met, Jay and I had gathered friends around a fire and read, "To Build a Fire" on winter's solstice. I travelled alone to his Beauty Ranch. Jay stayed behind to write.

Morning light veiled the Valley of the Moon as I sat in the dew-laden garden and pondered the closed-in porch of the sweet cottage where London had died. Sun's fiery globe rose through the trees. A spider web hung like a fairy rope from the nearest oak, swayed and bucked with the slightest breeze. *They had the perfect setup*, I mused. He lived on one side, his wife Charmian on the other. A Cooper's hawk circled and cried from above.

"I see my farm in terms of the world. I see the world in terms of my farm," he had written. His beloved land became his revolution.

I had no idea that after years of world travel the *Call of the Wild* author and unabashed Socialist turned his prolific energy from pen to earth. A Chinese-built stone barn protected his imported English Shire mares; an Italian-laid stone barn housed the stallions. My old farm dad would have chuckled at the state-of-the-art round "pig palace" built for registered Duroc Jersey pigs.

London raised the first stone block hollow silos in California and applied state-of-the-art farming techniques from around the world: terracing from Korea; crop rotation and nitrogen fixing from China. He dreamed of creating a utopian community that would provide for his family and workers as he penned a consistent thousand words a day.

Jack London died at 40. Years of alcohol abuse and self-administered morphine had seized his once sexy-strong body. Although he had kidney stones and rheumatism I figured he died of a broken heart. Writing critics had shunned his latest attempts, and he had recently found his prized Shire mare, in foal, shot dead in the field. His dream house, built to stand a thousand years, had mysteriously caught fire and burned to the ground just days before he and Charmian were due to move in.

He was buried beneath a simple gravestone on a hillside, his credo reverberating through the forest:

I would rather be ashes than dust!
I would rather that my spark should burn out in a brilliant blaze
Than it should be stifled by dryrot.
I would rather be a superb meteor,
Every atom of me in magnificent glow,
Than a sleepy and permanent planet.
The proper function of man is to live, not to exist.
I shall not waste my days in trying to prolong them.
I shall use my time.

I made my way up a trail across acres of vineyards through oak and redwood to London's high mountain pool. There were the remains of an old redwood bathhouse and an impressive stone dam. I could almost hear him and Charmian giggling as he chased her from the lake, catching her as they fell to the ground, entwined.

My mind turned to credos as I made my way down the mountain. Do women have credos? I didn't recall reading any. What would mine be? I began,

I believe in the power of silence.
The truth in the wild—

A huge bird swooped in front of me. I jumped to attention and recognized a pileated woodpecker. *Yeow!* I had never seen this bird before. He landed flamboyantly on a bunch of grapes left behind on a golden vine. He flapped and swooned as I realized with glee that the garrulous one was drunk on sun-fermented grapes.

Forty-Two

I craved time alone, wished I could have pitched a tent on the Beauty Ranch. I wanted to stop and let images ripen like grapes. Sit in oneiric space. I climbed into bed as I convinced myself it would happen in December in Arizona. I closed my eyes and tried to breathe but my nose was plugged. I sniffed, reached for a Kleenex and saw bright red. I had only had about five bloody noses in my life and this was my second one in three days. Jay had had one, too, earlier that day. He remembered them from his Berkeley days. "It's the Santa Ana winds," he said. "Put lotion in your nose. Keep it moist." Blood on the wings of wind.

I finally got to sleep and dreamed: "Jay, I think I'm dying," I said, as I fell peaceful by his side. The dream was so vivid it woke me up. The night before I'd dreamed I'd pressed the shutter on my camera and nothing happened. I surmised that the muse didn't like being put on hold.

It was our first Thanksgiving in Tortuga. The sweet smell of red cabbage gurgled away on the stove, grandma's recipe passed on from Aunt Clara. The day already was brimming with delight as two wild turkeys stretched their necks for acorns beneath the huge black oak. Here they were again, just in case I'd forgotten. They, oblivious to their millions of brothers and sisters that sat breast-up-featherless in roasting pans.

I luxuriated in an early morning hot tub amidst flitting California towhees, a tiny Kinglet and a lurking, longhaired cat who could only be named Scruffy. I spread a fresh coat of Teal for Two on my toenails and poured a second cup of coffee into the ceramic cup I had purchased with my daughter the day we trudged around the Pilar, New Mexico, art fair. I raised my cup to her in silent toast… imagined her sipping from hers at just that moment.

Red cabbage secured on the backseat floor, we headed toward the Oakland Hills and a Thanksgiving feast with Jay's old friend, John. There was no stopping us when we caught view of the Golden Gate Bridge. We decided to park and join the throngs of smiling families and hand-holding couples, face the wind and walk her glorious span.

And I was curious. *The San Francisco Chronicle* had just completed a week-long series on people who had jumped from the bridge, a collage of perspectives from those most touched: family and friends, counselors, and the first responders who pulled remains from the water in the rare event there was anything to retrieve.

The newspaper series was part of a community debate over whether the city should construct a barrier to thwart the final plunge that was said to take thirteen seconds before hitting the water. There were points raised yea and nay, but not a voice raised in defense of a person's right to end her life.

Walking across the bridge I saw bay and bird, rapturous blue sky and numerous attempts to change the suicidal mind. Phones were placed every few feet that connected to suicide hot lines and prominent signs pleaded with intent souls not to make the deadly leap. What became clear was this: to make the jump one had to be incredibly determined. First one had to *get* to the bridge which was miles from city center; then he had to take a long walk across the span. Finally a climb, first up, then over, then down to a lower level before one had a clear fall.

There was nothing romantic or effortless about this choice. This gleaming, haunting structure encapsulated the dark and the light. The bridge was a splendorous wonder, rendered even more authentic by the 80-year old woman who had turned her back on nursing home care and toppled toward the bay. A prayer was in order.

We made one more stop before we headed into Oakland—I was hankering for a walk along Berkeley's famed Telegraph Avenue. It had been years—twenty eight to be exact—since I had walked this street and bought a special pendant from a street vendor. It was an eye-catching emblem that prompted about one stranger a week to ask, "What *is* that?" Most thought it was a strange coin.

The imperfectly round silver circle was the size of a small quarter and it bore the imprint of a woman's head. The wind blew through her long hair as she looked toward a bird, perhaps a nightingale. An opal sat at the back of her slender neck. The feeling was undomesticated, Athena-like.

It was my spirit piece, and I wore it every day against my flesh. She had accompanied me on solo journeys into Guatemala's dark jungles, through six years of solitary life, up Colorado mountainsides, off the gringo trail in Mexico and into Zimbabwe's wild.

Alas, there were no vendors on Telegraph Avenue; no more revolutionary buzz. My hand-forged treasure would not have been found with the fast food bags wafting up the streets. Perhaps I shouldn't have returned. I passed on through, up the steep hill and through the iron gates of Berkeley's rose garden where I buried my nose into the coral pink Royal Dane rose.

Forty-Three

We were blessed by the weather Gods. The typical cool northern California rains had held off for our entire six-week sojourn. Now we looked south and east. Death Valley beckoned as we turned Tortuga around. We were even playing with the idea of Baja for the winter.

For the first time in our travels we were detoured by weather. Winter's first snowstorm blasted the Sierras as we headed for Tahoe, forcing us to turn around and head down the San Joaquin Valley. A windstorm blew clouds of alkali dust and sand from Owen's Valley Lake bed as we neared the turn for Death Valley. High profile vehicles were forced to pull over and wait for calm. We fired up the generator and made a lunch of popcorn. Took a nap. Made love and waited for the winds to change.

We pulled into Emigrant Campground as darkness fell. We hadn't planned to go that far but we were thrown off by the wind delay and couldn't find a place to boondock. Tortuga's brakes were hot and stinking from miles of long, steep twists and turns. Jay had geared down but to little avail. Relief exploded from our bodies when we stopped. We opened Tortuga's door and her steps unfolded as we scanned the stunning desolation of Death Valley, so vast and dramatic it mocked the camera. Why had it taken me 55 years to get there?

This valley, hot as the dickens in the summer, was lined with fans. Alluvial fans spread wide and round from the mouth of every canyon. Sculpted from rare rains that fell, they were formed by craggy mountains swept clean of any cover when floods of mud and rock poured onto the valley floor and left their shape in fans. Rivers of debris, frozen in time. Home to kingbird, red-tailed hawk, coyote, raven, roadrunner and desert bighorn. Home to the wind that scoured the scrawny greasewood.

A little kit fox appeared over the knoll as we prepared to turn in for the night. Pooka wasn't impressed.

We decided on Aguereberry Point for our first outing. It was a gravel road that led through a dry wash before it turned and headed up into the mountains. We figured it would give us a good overview. Once on the saddle we abandoned the car and climbed to a perch above the road that was out of the wind. We pulled out our lunches and watched as a large, faded sedan made its way up the precarious, steep, one-lane road. Took guts in *that* vehicle, I thought.

I expected adventuresome looking folk to pop out of that car. Instead there was an unhurried school marm carrying an Instamatic camera and a short, rotund oldster with a huge white beard, head topped with a straw hat. We waved hello from our point above and continued to munch away, taking in the view. The next time we glanced their way he was looking sadly down the cliff, his bald head reflecting sunlight like a mirror. He walked dejectedly to his car as the woman stayed put and continued to peer down.

Jay descended and took a look. The hat hadn't fallen far but it was on a steep scree cliffside. Jay, with his wide leg span, made four careful stretch-steps to retrieve the hat. Marm showered us in thanks as she explained that her husband had Bell's palsy. Direct sunlight was dangerous; thus his hasty retreat to the car. She scurried back to the car, hat in hand. The little fat man never reappeared. We continued to explore around the mountain on foot as they drove away.

I was turning the key in the ignition when I noticed a piece of paper under the windshield wiper. Jay grabbed it and handed it to me with a big grin. It was a business card with a picture of our friend, straw hat exchanged for a bright red stocking cap that dangled beside his bushy, snow white beard. *Greetings From Santa* read the card. On the back in ballpoint ink was scribbled, *Thanks for retrieving my hat.*

We were closing in on winter's solstice. It was dark by 4:30 and I was snuggled into bed by 8:00. To read. To ponder the unimaginable of this place. Slot canyons that looked to be painted in huge black African textile stripes. Picasso walls of inlayed rock in small geometric triangles and squares. Smooth-shine milky rose marble that beckoned me to lie down and slide.

One moment I was born anew, the next I stood exposed at dawn, 200-feet below sea level. It was 134-degrees at Badwater in the summer but I was chilled in a sweater, down vest, gloves and a winter hat. We headed out onto the flat valley floor of the white salt crystals. There were no trees on this endless expanse. No rock, nothing to anchor the mind. It didn't take long to lose one's bearings, to be lost in a white-out of stifling silence, frozen grasshoppers and a dead fly or two.

The languages of silence were many.

Grand Canyon silence droned and pressed and made me small.

Zion silence bounced through rock chambers.

Bryce silence swooshed among hoo-doos.

Silence leaned. It freed. It sometimes constrained. But always, always she joined the soul in spirit duet.

Silence, the endangered species. My redeemer.

Teach children the power of silence and they will never want for places to feed the soul.

We sat on the dirt at the famed scenic pullout named Artist's Palette, a tasty cigar and our flask of port in hand. A slim blond guy decked out in LL Bean made his way over. At least five grands worth of digital camera dangled huge around his neck. Turned out he was a photographer from the *LA Times* working up a travel feature. A chunky young woman came along next and joined us. She chugged a beer as she shared her exploits of a solo cross-country trip. She was on her way home to New Zealand.

It was the four of us, a little port, raucous laughs and the setting sun. Deep reds and greens and chocolate browns. Venus ruled from on high in radiant sparkle as Mr. Times snapped shots and told us we'd soon be in the paper. Our two seconds of fame.

That afternoon Dad came to me in a dream in the middle of a nap.

I understand, he said, in a booming voice full of love.

It woke me straight up.

I understand. It bore the healing weight of a thousand lifetimes.

I dreamt of him more as he grew older. Otto Henry Nealson was nearing ninety years old and he was quick to tell me that it was nothing to celebrate, his deep voice and boisterous laugh forever his trademark.

The old Dane was a man of few words and fewer still expressions of love. He telephoned me once in my entire life. I'd sent him my first published book, and when he finished reading it he picked up the phone and called. "I'm so proud of you," he said.

I understand, he had said. What did he know that I did not?

Death Valley, the place of the profound empty.

Forty-Four

We moved toward Naco and Christmas plans with Em and Paul. On the way was Quartzite, a humongous RV bazaar and wintering grounds for tens of thousands of snowbirds. Quartzite was a small town surrounded by thousands of acres of BLM lands designated for camping. You could dry camp up to six months for a couple hundred bucks.

Things didn't really get buzzing until January when they hosted the largest RV show in the country, a huge gem and mineral gathering and acres of flea market booths that sold anything you could possibly want. The scale was daunting as we walked long, tent-studded rows to collect some things on our wish list. We found a truck antenna for our rig to strengthen our cell phone signal and a nifty protector to wrap around our grill to protect the flame from the wind. I even found a jeweler who replaced the opal on my wild woman necklace.

Two nights was about all we could take of Quartzite's treeless desert and dust. And for the first time in her life Belle was sick, throwing up her food. For months she'd been slowing down. It was harder and harder for her to get up the stairs and she no longer kept up on hikes. She also had trouble swallowing and she peed a lot. She was a few weeks away from her 10th birthday. For a 110-pound dog that's around age 80. I made an appointment with a Quartzite vet.

The vet checked Belle's vitals, drew some blood from her leg and found that her kidney function was okay. The sweet older man didn't believe it was time to take drastic measures and prescribed a low-protein food specifically for old dogs, canned and dry. I broke out in tears of relief.

We pulled into Em and Paul's a few days before winter solstice. We set the little pine we had taken from the earth in Death Valley into a container of rock and water and placed her in Tortuga. Yes, I know. We weren't supposed to take a tree from Death Valley. But Santa had just left a note on our windshield when we saw this foot-high piñon in a wide, sandy arroyo. It would have survived only until the next flash flood.

I strung our small colored lights around Tortuga's innards and hung our decorations from the cord. It was our first Christmas season as full-timers. I loved the sparkle and comfort of the decorations I'd collected over the years. I'd chosen around 20 to save: a ceramic model of an old pickup, a wooden goddess, a glass magpie. The ones I hadn't saved I had mailed to Hope to kick-start her ritual of decorations.

Tortuga decked out, I began to bake. Danish pebernoder, ginger snaps and mincemeat cookies. My ultra-rich piñon nut fudge. I took comfort in comfort food and my holiday rituals. It was the only time of year I devoured white sugar.

I savored the darkness of winter solstice. Darkness as prerequisite to light. Death as forbearer to life. On solstice-eve we built a fire in the back yard and took turns reading from London's "To Build a Fire."

A half-hour's drive from Naco was a magic little place called Whitewater Draw in the middle of a desolate valley, another non-sexy favorite. The four of us bundled up on solstice morning and joined forty thousand sandhill cranes packed to the brim into shallow ponds. There were myriad shovelers and coots and a distant dollop of snow geese. Dark clouds of roosting yellow-headed blackbirds rattled the rushes like angry spirits.

Extraordinary Whitewater Draw was the perfect solstice choice. The cranes began to stir with flaps of wing. A screech owl perched in a scrubby mesquite a few arms' length away, blinked heavy into dawn. Her feathers fluffed against crystalline cold that numbed my gloved fingers. Praise be! The sun turned north in her cyclical journey of hope.

I pulled the blue spotted roaster out of its oven hidey hole. A hand-me-down from mom, it was one of the large, heavy things I had refused to jettison. It carried memories of holidays and now it would hold a stuffed and roasted 12-pound turkey on Christmas day.

The sweet-vinegary smell of red cabbage filled the air. Em and Paul brought mashed potatoes and pumpkin chiffon pie for our first formal dinner within Tortuga's walls. All felt complete as we neared our one year anniversary of this life.

Belle had good days and she had bad days. She kept the canned food down but had trouble swallowing. She went with me on short walks and then collapsed and slept for hours. I was desperate for answers as I contemplated putting her down. I researched the Internet where I read how dogs live longer these days than they normally would, and how, by the time they show pain, the pain is great. Dogs are stoics.

I watched Belle closely, determined not to keep her alive for my sake. Mexico loomed and I did not want Belle to die there, where I would have to leave her behind. I returned to Whitewater Draw on the dark of moon to take solace with avocet and ruddy duck, teals and pintails. I looped around the water's edge and dipped into the woods. A Cooper's hawk swayed low. Deeper into the timber heart I walked, followed a deer path over logs through thick undergrowth. A barn owl departed its limb in a flash of white and skirted above me in silent flight. I stretched to watch where it landed. Breathed the rich, cool silence.

Standing still as death I sensed movement and strained to see into the tangled mass of vines and leaves. On a dead, fallen limb about six feet above the ground sat the Cooper's hawk. Two feet away, on the same fallen trunk, sat a statuesque long-eared owl.

I was stung with disbelief. It was the proverbial lion and the lamb.

Belle struggled into the back seat of the car and her walks became slow and slower. She only occasionally rose to her spunky self. She had four bad days to one good one. It. Was. Time. I said goodbye for a week. Took her for walks. Sat with her under trees. Asked her understanding.

She was having none of it. I was on my own.

So hard, that day. Once roused she perked up: walked and peed and took a little dump. Barked at Maya, Emilie's dog, and looked at me so pleased. Then she wanted back into Tortuga. It was not to be. I directed her to the car where I sat in the back seat with her while Jay drove.

For all her gentle love she did not go gently into the night. She would not give her paw to the vet. I sat with her, leaned my head to the left, over hers. I talked to her and held her tight as the needle entered her foot and the deadly serum raced through her veins. Belle let loose with a long loud yowl and I broke out in sobs. Oh my god. I squeezed her hard. It was death that tore us apart.

All was numbness and tears, a gaping hole in my heart and my chest afire. I tried to connect with that olden-day wise woman whose role was to give death on behalf of the tribe. Her energy was with me as the needle slid; then she took a powder.

Belle Negra's grave faced north, and I buried her with the "love your mother" cap that I had made and worn years ago for the Rocky Flats encirclement. I built a stone altar and lit a candle. There was no more pain for Belle. No more boredom or indignation. For me, no more deep brown eyes of love. No more companion. No more snores to fill the hearth and home. Roo-roo-roo, her happy bark. Ruf, the sound of protection. Ah-oooooooh, so happy to be with you.

Jay and I lowered her into the grave on a blanket; then I drove down the road and howled back to her. Within the confines of the car, I screamed my loss. My daemon, gone. I made a list of those who love me as if to fill the hole she left behind.

Met the owl and the hawk face on.

We decided to head toward Baja. It made no sense to linger at Belle's grave. Death permeated my presence. My bleeding body, thirty years in sync with the moon's cue to receive sperm and gestate flesh, now sputtered and died to that intent. I, cast adrift in a vast hormonal tide.

My written words derailed by grief, the word odyssey blinked upon my radar.

Forty-Five

Imagine a cat sitting upright. Now imagine that cat lowering her head forward, resting it between her front paws and closing her eyes as if in sleep or meditation. Or perhaps mourning? This was the position Pooka took up on the dash of Tortuga following Belle's death. She, my spotted Buddha.

Entry into Mexico was thankfully easy and quick. We'd done the prep and had passports, vehicle titles and proof of insurance at hand. A vet certified certificate of good health for the animals. Correction, animal. We also had the time to wait in line and get the proper stickers for vehicle windows. You do all that and then you pray for the green light that will signal you onward without a search. I'd never gotten a red light and this entry was no exception.

Viva Mexico! Twenty-five years of visits and I still let loose with a huge breath of joy. The change in tenor between the two countries was palpable. Immediate color, wider smiles, peoples that operated on simple, familial levels. US friends reacted with shock that I would pack up and head south, concerned for my safety and the mythical banditos. I'm not saying they didn't exist; I'm saying that in my years of solo bus travel and hitchhiking across Mexico and Central America I had never been hassled. Just the same, although I was confident about Mexico, I wasn't as sure about driving a motorhome south of the border. I was no longer milling with the people; I was above them. Literally. This is where RV guidebooks came in handy. I had two at my side, carefully outlining the route, stops and parks along the way.

Miles of sand dune and ocean, is how the guidebook described El Pabellon RV Park. *And not much else.* The book was right on both counts. One mile of sandy road from the highway, it turned out to be a sweet place of minimalist beauty. The few buildings were cement block painted in bright greens and yellows. A whale skeleton served as the centerpiece of meager landscaping. A plump little Mexican woman made her way into the driveway and began to jabber away in Spanish. It was a little nerve wracking. I didn't understand her! *How* much money to stay? *What* were her directions? I took a deep breath and realized I only had to say, "*Habla mas despacio, por favor*. Speak more slowly, please, whereupon I understood the prices and directions just fine. Another big hurdle.

The oceanfront parking places were windows on the divine. Dunes and small trees separated us from two fellow RV'ers. There was central water, a minimal dump station and miles of undeveloped beach. It was $3 for the night. It was isolated but felt safe.

Mexican Tortuga adjustments were minimal. A few spoonsful of Clorox in our water tank guaranteed potable water. Our indoor filter took away the taste and smell of bleach. The other preparations we had made were perfect, like the solar panel that collected energy to keep us in power and run the holy coffee grinder.

I walked for hours amidst sand dollars and shells as the ceaseless ocean worked her hypnotic ways. I cried a lot, wondering how long it would take for the gaping hole left by Belle's death to dissipate. Meanwhile, Pooka did her darnedest to fill the void. She took to playing fetch and followed me around like... well, a dog.

Endless beach was the perfect introduction to the Baja but we longed for warmer climes. That meant heading below the Tropic of Cancer. After three days on the ocean we cranked the ignition and headed south on Baja's only primary road, a thousand-mile ribbon of asphalt, so far, pothole free.

Our first stop of the day was lunch, when we pulled off the highway and parked on a dirt street in the village of El Rosario. I'd read about Mama Espinoza's lobster burritos in the guidebook and we weren't going to pass them up! Neither did thirty others. The tiny place even had Internet. I didn't know whether to feel relived or chagrinned; disconnecting from the world felt more appropriate on the Baja.

We pulled onto the highway; relieved that we'd successfully stopped and parked Tortuga along the road. We were adjusting well to our environs, camping, reading menus, ordering. I was just thinking how Tortuga's size wasn't going to be a problem when the highway narrowed, leaving only a few inches of space between passing trucks and our mirrors. As if to up the ante, the shoulders disappeared. Then the white lines that designated the side of the road went away. Myriad side mirror parts were strewn along the way. I bordered on panic. Jay was silent, in deep concentration as he gripped the wheel with sweaty hands.

This, as the Baja-scape opened into a glorious desert of queer, exotic plants. I was transported to the bottom of the sea in Lewis Carroll fashion. Boojums sprouted from the ground like upside-down carrots. The giant cardon, a sahuaro-like cactus, dwarfed its northern cousin. There were weird yuccas, the likes of which I'd never seen, century plants, chollas and boulders the size of small houses. Of course there weren't any places to pull over. Baja demanded a schizophrenic state of mind as it simultaneously served up the extremes of good and bad.

If I had been Catholic, I would have screamed a few Hail Marys as we pulled into our next camp. Relief didn't begin to describe my entry into another simple park in a beautiful place, although it wasn't as straightforward as the night before. No one was around to take money, designate a space or give directions; we took our cues from the other few campers and parked. With the sun falling fast, we took off for a walk into the desert hills as the pain of Belle's death spiked high inside. No dog to lope along, I brushed tears away and shot some pictures of Jay in the backlit boojum forest.

We were headed back to camp when the air filled with "Ain't Too Proud to Beg," as a gringo cheerleader roused a travel-weary audience through a portable microphone. Cheers, laughter and dancing commenced. It was my first exposure to American RV-caravans and I was irked. The tent campers couldn't believe their bad luck. We'd traveled solo all those miles to experience Mexico; we wouldn't have minded Mexican music. We went it alone while caravaners sought safety in numbers. I guessed they were people who normally wouldn't have come down the Baja and they felt protected in a large group. They kept to a regimented schedule, secure within their mobile community.

Lucky for us the caravan was headed north the next morning. We met another one midmorning, a line of twenty-five snaking slowly down the road. From that day forward I checked the descriptions of the camps to see whether they were big enough to accommodate caravans. Then we chose another.

Forty-Six

When does journey become odyssey?

I'm talking soul. Something akin to a parallel universe into which we dip and risk, perhaps, no return. Our place on this cusp can begin as any other day but when we look back, we see that our entire life led us to that point.

We stopped in the small city of Guerrero Negro, excited to buy our first Baja lobster, shrimp and scallops at a seafood store mentioned in one of my guidebooks. That's where the wooden billboard caught my eye. It announced gray whales and boat tours on Laguna Ojo de Liebre. I checked the maps. We weren't that far from the shores of the Scammon's Lagoon where gray whales migrated from the waters off Alaska, and there was primitive camping. We were game.

The 15-miles of gravel and dirt two-track went from smooth-packed alkali to teeth-shaking stutter bumps. I doubted the wisdom of our spontaneity about the time the knife rack came off the wall and I heard the clink of broken glass in the cupboard.

Once at the lagoon we found a camping spot at water's edge. The only one, it turned out, that could have accommodated Tortuga's size. We unpacked as song sparrows trilled from the scrub; shorebirds floated and dipped along the gentle shore. I couldn't wipe the smile off my face as I leashed up Pooka and started down a narrow two-track that followed the shore. That's when I saw my first whale—a gray, sleek body that heaved from the sea; 45 feet of straight up, lean and splash. The bay brimmed with churning whales at dusk. The haunting sound of spouting water rose through the darkness all night long.

It wasn't my intent to boat into the lagoon. I didn't want to bother the whales. This was their birthing lagoon and I'd never been keen on boatfuls of tourists. But by the next afternoon the throngs of sightseers had returned by van to Guerro Negro and a little boat sat empty on the shore. I was overtaken with excitement and just like that we were seated in the panga with a couple from France. They were in their 70's. Fellow adventurers, they'd flown into LA, rented a car and were driving down the Baja. Our bright blue panga took to the waters awash in Spanish, French and English babble. Within twenty minutes we were surrounded by the giant ones.

Enrique, our boatman, spoke little English. He told us that the recent census had counted 1500 gray whales in the bay. I didn't think to ask whether that was more or less than last year. "They live to be 50-60 years old," he said.

The males sky-hopped and spouted from a distance as mothers and calves stayed near. The babes were five or six weeks old, said Enrique. I watched mesmerized as they swam at their mamas' sides, rolling beside them, over them, never apart. Art in motion. Gentle and beautiful, the moms and calves moved closer.

I was full as any moment in my life and ready to turn toward shore when events said otherwise. One mother picked up speed, calf at her side, and headed for our boat. Wonder turned to fear when it was clear she wasn't going to stop. I tensed against a ram and gripped the sides of the boat as she dove under our seats at the last moment. It was a fake charge that hearkened back to a rhino in Zimbabwe and pee-my-pants terror. I'd never climbed a tree so fast. No trees out here.

I tightened my life vest as I caught sight of her again. Once more, she came at us and under. Were they playing with us? They picked up steam again and then suddenly slowed, came to the side of the boat and stopped. I leaned over toward them as she lifted from the water and edged her gargantuan head toward my splashing hand. Her huge eye held the universe. I reached to her and touched. She was sleek and soft, goddess and god, the ultimate of holies.

Time dissolved as she stayed with my hand. An eternity wrapped in motion. Then she dipped below, circled and returned again with her calf. Little One had a deep wrinkle on its forehead, an ineffable aura of sweetness and power. Mama whale had the four of us just where she wanted us, bent over and awestruck, when she let loose with a spout of water and a blow that backed us up in shrieks of laughter. And just like that, she was gone, our deserted panga rocking gently in the vast, silent lagoon.

The most remarkable feeling of completion swept through me. I could die now.

Forty-Seven

Thousands of people travelled down the Baja to witness the whales. I assumed everyone got to touch them. Not so. Touch-me visitations were rare, although there were recently more accounts of it happening.

Scammon's Lagoon was named for Charles Melville Scammon, who tracked the whales into their protected birthing inlet in the 1850s. He slaughtered them nearly to extinction. I flashed on the other gray giants I had witnessed, the elephants of Zimbabwe, under assault for their ivory.

The elephant was not as forgiving of attacks against family. A mother elephant did not forget the face of her attacker and was known to avenge acts of violence years after they took place. The watery whale took a different tact. Barnacled-She rose from the ocean and looked into my eyes. She forged a miraculous bond.

From this point on, the highway down the peninsula took on the significance of a birth canal. I was only a couple of hours from the moon-tugged ocean from anywhere on the Baja. Seventy percent of the earth was covered in ocean. Seventy percent of my body was water. Human life began with nine months of float, of breathing underwater in my mother's belly through gills.

I had touched the beings who filled the depths with sound and song; I had been eye-to-eye with wit and wisdom. It was a gift that carried responsibility. I didn't have answers but the visits of turkey, moose and whale leaned heavy on the soul.

Leaving that lagoon of life—the sounds and smells and touch of whale flesh—was one of the hardest things I have ever done. Tortuga rocked and bumped her way once more across the salt flats as needy natives stood along the road holding out chunks of salt for sale. Since our arrival I had learned that these white lands were called the Essa Salt Works and they were the focus of a heated environmental battle to close the operation that threatened the birthing lagoon. The spirit of Scammon came in many forms. This time, the whales had won. But they weren't stopping at that, were they?

Forty-Eight

We crossed the peninsula and headed down the Gulf side. Tight winding roads with no shoulders or lines served up a rude, final hurrah: sheer cliff dropoffs. I found out firsthand why the passenger seat was called the suicide seat in the Baja. Every time we met a semi-truck or rounded a blind curve I clenched the arm rest and closed my eyes. I was in a constant state of hyper-alert. I jerked from time to time in fear and it drove Jay crazy. I shrilly warned him when Tortuga's tires clung to the crumbled asphalt. He got pissed and I returned the sentiment. His wine glass filled again to the brim. Anger on top of stress. It wasn't good.

We stopped in the palm-filled town of Mulege long enough to know we wanted to stay awhile. A river village near the sea, it brimmed with fishermen and all the practical things we needed like a laundry and a Mexican grocery store. We traveled about 20-miles south to a little spot on Bahia Concepcion called La Perla where we came pretty close to never leaving.

There were many camping areas on the Bay of Concepción. One even had full hook-ups. All were scenic and some accommodated the lucrative train of American-driven RV's. La Perla had a hidden sandy turnoff where Jay pulled over and waited while I got out and walked. When I rounded the curve and looked down on the small inlet I couldn't believe the bucolic beauty. The two-track was narrow and bit scrubby with a sharp turn thrown in but I surmised we could make it.

Rosa was the hunched-over wiry mother and grandmother who ruled the family lands. Folks said she was around fifty years old but she wore the tired, leathered look of seventy. Rosa rented out six palapa-dotted spots to campers like us on her little inlet. She charged five dollars a day to park a few feet from the water, mountains fore and aft. At dawn her fisherman sons took their small motorboat into the Sea of Cortez. Late morning their wives drove into Rosa's in their beat-up car, toddlers in tow. They sat outside together and talked the day away while they awaited the fishermen's return.

Rosa stood outside of her dirt-floored shack, a touching scene as she mixed and patted tortillas and cooked them on top of her stove, a forty-gallon metal drum under which she had started a fire. The men returned in the early afternoon and handed over their catch to the women, who cleaned the fresh scallops and shrimp. A couple of hours later they came around and sold them to us, the lucky ones, for fifty pesos a kilo. That's five dollars for a little over two pounds.

We made quick friends with our palapa neighbors. There was Dave, a big-hearted, big-bodied guy who had left his girlfriend behind in Truth or Consequences, New Mexico. (First American RV'er we'd met not attached to a caravan!) Eve set up home in one of the palapas alongside her VW van. She was from British Columbia, making her first solo trip since her husband died. They had journeyed for years to this special place every winter. Now she came with his ashes where she would leave him behind in his favorite earthly place. And they kept rolling in… Patricia, Ellen a few days later. All Canadians.

One day rolled seamlessly into the next. Spectacular sunrises were followed by beat-up trucks of Mexicanos bearing fresh fruits and vegetables. Pork and beef tamales. Pineapple turnovers. One year into our motorhome life I walked La Perla's snuggly bay at night, bio-luminescence thick as tide froth. I lazed and read and wrote, occasionally starting up the car to discover the many inlet nooks of Bahia de Concepción. The cliffside highway wound its way along the water's edge in dramatic roller-coaster fashion, allotting views of sand, water, rock and palms.

I had wondered, before we crossed the border, whether we should take the Honda. The extra length, the expense; simplicity might have been much easier in undeveloped Baja. But once down the road it afforded us trips to places we never would have seen otherwise. Jay and I ventured into Mulege for Valentine's Day and pulled up a seat in a salty dive where fresh oysters mingled with weathered fishermen hunched over the bar who looked right out of Hemingway. The Baja was everything I'd hoped. Memorable scenes were everywhere: children playing basketball, a piano hoisted up the side of building, swaying palms and seafood at every turn.

"Would you like to go out and meet the dolphins?" Dave asked one sleepy afternoon. We'd been watching them leap their way through distant waters every day. He didn't have to ask twice. Twenty minutes later we were in his boat, zipping along beside a playful pod of twelve who raced and leapt beside the boat. When we stopped they approached, waited for our next acceleration, then took off with us again, criss-crossing in front of us and circling back, an exhilarating game.

Nights unfurled on La Perla's little beach in the wake of brandy-swilling, guitar-picking rounds. Gentle breezes fed the fire as soft, receding waves left lines of neon-green luminescence on the shore. We closed out the hootenanny with, "And it's one, two, three what are we fighting fooooooor? Don't ask me I don't give a damn. Next stop is Viet Nam." Country Joe and the Fish echoed softly from the hidden banks of "The Pearl."

Forty-Nine

By now we were thinking we'd travel to the end of the Baja, loop around the Cape and return north. We pulled into La Paz on Mardi Gras and all the camps were full. Because we were staying only one night, however, there was one spot available, held for someone coming in the next day. Carnival was a riot of color, loud bands every few feet and booths of Mexican pastries, brown sugar shapes and glazed fruits. In other words, sugar, sugar and... well, sugar. We walked the promenade hand-in-hand as giggly teenage girls approached and asked for my permission to have their picture taken with Jay. He, the handsome gringo star. And yes he was. Why didn't I feel it? We were moving down the Baja, superb, lust-less travel partners.

The next day we landed on Baja's southern tip, well below the Tropic of Cancer and its promise of hot, sunny days. Los Cerritos beach was an expansive boondock and popular surfing spot between Cabo and Todos Santos. We decided to stay a month. We strayed beyond the noisy surfing beach and camped amidst hundreds of— you know what I'm going to say—Canadians. The pattern was clear. While Americans stayed above the border imagining banditos around every Mexican corner, the Canadians turned out the lights and headed solo to the Baja beaches. *They* believed that the U.S. was the most dangerous part of the trip.

The waters were warm, the beaches long and white with a constant supply of good ganja. The main supplier was a washed-up construction worker from California, the self-appointed sheriff of the beach, given to fits of screaming in the middle of the night. I kept a friendly distance. He made me nervous, as did a young hippie couple from British Columbia on the other side of us who were stoned and paranoid 24/7 as they peeked out their curtained windows. Oh, they seemed friendly enough when they managed to say a few words, but violent arguments erupted between them from time to time. I wasn't afraid, just wary.

Their presence was more than balanced out by the arrival of Jan and De. Middle-aged adventurers like ourselves, they'd landed in LA from their Australia home, bought a truck and camper and ended up parked behind us. Jan took to his surf board at least once a day while De and I sat, yakked and watched. He was a jolly sight, his muffin-top hanging over his boxer swim trunks. Jay—where was Jay? Working on his book, making trips for water, walking, snorkeling. Our some-sex marriage limped along.

Baja spoke best through her simple images and stories. Like three tiny gecko eggs hatched inside a door latch; or the minute campesino on an isolated homestead in the mountains of Sierra de la Laguna.

We had traveled a narrow two-track, barely more than a cow path, through cactus and thorn brush. The road was getting fainter and fainter as I grew more nervous. There we were in the Baja mountains, isolated and far away from any possible assistance should anything go wrong. I could almost see the buzzards circling as we rounded a blind corner and chickens (they were all loose on the Baja!) clucked and scattered.

The road and our escapade ended at a dilapidated collection of corrals. A scrawny hog took cover as we turned around. We stopped next to the aged man who sat bent over on a dilapidated wooden stool, milking a bony cow. Like Rosa before, it was hard to tell how old he was.

He'd wrapped a soft cord around the cow's hind legs to prevent an errant kick. He knew where he was. We didn't. This was not our destination of La Candelaria. He gave us directions in a rapid-fire strange dialect of Spanish that we managed to decipher. We had to return to the highway, continue east and turn up a wash. And yes, he answered with a shy smile, it was okay to take his picture. My heart opened wide as I snapped the little man with a dirty rope belt around his waist and his dented bucket of warm, frothy milk.

We headed back down the mountain as I mined the metaphors of the excursion. There was no such thing as a dead end. I mustn't get too hung up on the idea of destinations. Pretty darned close to *You can not chase what is meant to be.*

Fifty

We made it to La Candelaria that day. My guidebook told me I was going to see picturesque village homes of *curanderas*, medicine women who worked with herbs, but I was stymied. We'd followed the farmer's directions and ventured up a precipitous two-track with frightening blind corners. I was breathless and relieved to finally come to a cluster of scattered houses. Nothing, however, pointed to a place of interest. Determined to connect with someone who might give us directions, I followed a faded, hand-painted sign that said *Potter* to a cactus-spine gate on the side of the hill.

On the gate was a second sign that instructed one to ring the cow bell. A hearty clang filled the air. There was no response so I shook the old bell again. The house was a ways down the hill and I wondered whether they could hear the bell. Jay and I stood in the hot sun and waited. After an extended Baja minute a quiet, large-boned gringa lumbered up the hill in our direction. "Hi," she said with a strange combination of shyness and power. "I'm Lorena."

Great, I thought. *So much for mystical Mexican healers.*

Lorena led us slowly down the hill with the air of a disciple. We ended up in an open-roofed room where she offered us a seat on straw, high-backed chairs. She wanted to know our names and where we were from. She told us that if we were after pots she had none. Despite her isolation, people found their way to her and bought her pots as fast as she could create them. She mentioned two clay gems, however, that were curing in the sun and not ready for sale. That was no problem. We hadn't come for pots. In fact, I wasn't sure *why* we were there, listening to Lorena, surrounded by a flourish of flowers and fist-sized butterflies air-dancing about.

Lorena picked up a small, flat stone, dipped it in water and began to slide it back and forth over a soft, clay pot. Then she began to speak, accompanied by the hypnotic dip and smooth and a new-born pot of satin sheen. She told us that she was the only white person who lived in La Candelaria. Eighteen years ago she had visited the Baja from her home in Portland, Oregon, and she'd never left. She had been in search of a place to immerse herself in the Spanish language. Her friend dropped her off with a family in the village and that was that. "If you want to learn Spanish, take a Mexican lover." Her soft laugh mingled with the distant tinkling of hundreds of goats' bells. *Chuparosas* (hummingbirds) zipped past our heads; bees swayed and hummed their way toward nectar as life fell into trance.

Lorena married her lover, Ernesto. As she prepared for a final trip to Portland, she asked Ernesto whether there was anything he desired from the United States. He didn't pause a moment. "Una pistola," he said. And so, when she packed her camper to move to La Candelaria she included her contraband. She gave the gun to him and in return he gave her a cow. He asked that he be given the male calves and she would keep the females. Fair enough, she said.

She named the cow La Pistola, and for the next six years the cow had only female calves. In the end she gave them back to her lover. She said she didn't really need cows, except for the cow patties she used as fuel to fire her pots.

An enchanting silence enveloped us as we listened to this woman, queen of pots and gardens.

I asked, "Lorena, could I see the two pots that are curing?"

We walked across the hill where they laid in the sun, the color of red earth. The smaller one was called a *casuelita* (little bowl). It resembled a jewel.

"Could I buy this pot and return to pick it up?" The words were out of my mouth before I had time to think. Come back? It had taken hours to find this place. Her eyebrows rose as she answered. "Yes." So it was I purchased the little pot full of grace and signed us up for another venture into La Candelaria. It was the first art I had been moved to possess since we had taken to the road. Call me crazy. I'd just bought a piece of pottery for a motorhome life where lightweight, non-breakable ruled.

Not to worry, Lorena said. Her pots contained high sand content in the clay. "My pots do not break easily," she said. "They bounce. You can put them directly on the flame because the firing takes the water out of them. It's the fire that turns them black and creates the whirls in the patina."

We turned to leave as I mentioned to Lorena that we had ventured up to La Candelaria in search of curanderas. She let loose with a guffaw and said that was a myth the guidebooks print. Nearing the gate she pointed out the pit where she burned her pots in the manure of La Pistola's descendants. She said the clay for her pots came from her land. That she dug between the new and full moon.

"By the way," she said. "Take that road back." She pointed in the opposite direction from which we'd arrived. But if we'd found the main road to begin with we wouldn't have found Lorena, situated deep in the bowels of the village. I smiled as I reviewed the day… the hunches and supposedly wrong turns that had delivered me to nothing short of magic.

Sure, Lorena… there were no curanderas in La Candelaria.

Fifty-One

To the north of Los Cerritos was Todos Santos, an artsy village that many Americans called home until the heat set in about April. To the south was Cabo San Lucas, where cruise ships and jet planes dumped tourists by the hundreds. The good news was that we found picturesque little inlets filled with colorful fish for the snorkeling eye. The bad news was that just when we'd spread our blankets in solitary bliss, in roared a tour boat, music blaring, to drop off several dozen snorkelers.

We were three weeks into our boondock when I received an email from girlfriend Susan in Taos. Her sister-in-law in Todos Santos needed a house sitter in March and wondered whether we'd like to park there. We were intrigued and arranged to meet Larry and Laurel.

Todos was their second home. Larry commuted to his Santa Fe law practice while Laurel anchored on the Baja, painting and tending to community volunteer projects. We met over Laurel's fresh guacamole and tortillas and took an immediate liking to one another. Most importantly, Tortuga would fit. Their mango-laden lands were within sight of the ocean. Jay made several trips to prune mesquite along the rutted two-track that led to their driveway.

We were a few days from moving when spiking pain began to radiate from my neck, into my shoulders and down my arms. What was *this*? It continued for days and nothing made it go away. Not a trip into Cabo to a chiropractor. Not a teary goodbye letter to Belle to free residual grief in the confines of my muscles. I paid an old clairvoyant hippie on the beach for a massage, who muttered away about how he felt something strange in my neck. As if to tease, the pain moved from one shoulder to the other. I dreamt of Quetzalcoatl, Feathered One, plumed serpent descendent of the meso-America people. He enveloped me in an eclipse. Darkened the skies and raised the winds.

I watched in deep frustration as moving day drew near. The access road to the house-sit was closed by a detour that involved steep, dirt hills and ruts, a paving job that was several months behind deadline. Mañana-Mexico. A pain in the neck. I scouted an alternative route in the Honda and we eventually pulled into the house, tense but unscathed. Larry and Laurel gave us the tour and introduced us to the various tasks of *Rancho Siempre Algo*, the Always Something Ranch, as in there was always something that needed to be fixed.

We parked by a sweet, woven gazebo surrounded by Laurel's gardens of flowers, herbs and vegetables. Trees hung heavy with avocado and papaya. They harvested five varieties of bananas, including Cuban reds, small scarlet crescents on the vine. We planned three weeks at our little piece of heaven on the outskirts of Todos Santos, home to the renowned Hotel California, where the Eagles had warned, you could never leave. I found out why that night, when I got so drunk drinking their Damiana margaritas that I couldn't lower myself off the six-foot high barstool. Well okay, not six feet, but at least four. It looked to be one hell of a long way down. Damiana was a local plant and lauded aphrodisiac. I figured it was worth a try. Instead, Jay and I both passed out.

Next door to Rancho Siempre Algo was a 20-foot travel trailer that neighbor Steve called home. A middle-aged California transplant, he'd swapped his name for the Spanish version, Esteban, and proceeded in his search to find a Mexican wife. He paid $120 a month to park on a little piece of land where he created metal sculptures of skinny spirit figures with long, pointy breasts.

Thus far Esteban lived alone and hadn't been successful in his wife quest. It had been rough going, right down to his attempt to get a dog, which seemed a little odd since stray dogs were everywhere in Mexico, usually with a litter of pups hidden away. The Baja told her own particular tale.

Esteban *had* mentioned to his Mexican landlord he was thinking of getting a dog. News travels fast *en Mexico*. It wasn't long before an unkempt drunk weaved up to his gate, claiming to be the landlord's friend. "Here's your dog," he blurted, as he pointed to a

Boxer covered in fresh cuts and scars. Estaban wasn't so sure. "Take her," coaxed the disheveled man. "She's free."

Esteban looked at the forlorn animal with protruding ribs. "Well, okay," he said.

"Her name is Chatta," said the drunk.

"What does it mean?" asked Esteban.

"Nothin'. Just a name." He handed Chatta's dirty rope to Esteban, nodded, and asked to borrow 100 pesos for a beer.

Free. Right.

Shy Chatta filled out on several weeks of dog food and table scraps; her cuts healed. She and Esteban became inseparable as Chatta learned to trust a caring voice while Esteban slowly gave his heart to the four-legged creature with inquisitive eyes. He was no longer alone and had to admit it felt good. The highlight of the day was when Chatta accompanied Esteban on his daily four-mile run along the Pacific and down the two-track side street of Todos Santos, stopping at a tienda to buy Chatta a dog treat.

It was on one such run that Esteban was dreaming his next sculpture when from a distance someone hollered, "Daisy! *Dais-y*! Is that you?"

Esteban ignored the call and kept running. "Daisy! Here Daisy!" Esteban pulled up short and turned to see Chatta's donor a half-block away standing next to another man who slapped his legs and continued to call out. It slowly dawned on Esteban as he turned around. Had the drunk given him another man's dog? Chatta shuddered with excitement as she looked at Esteban then toward the man calling out for Daisy.

"Well Chatta," Esteban said as he rubbed her behind the ears. "What do you want?" Surely she wouldn't return to the man who had beaten her. Chatta glanced one last time at Esteban, then bounded away in the direction of the voice as Esteban stared after her and turned away when he couldn't stand it anymore.

Esteban changed his running route and fed Chatta's dog food to the birds. He never saw her again and resumed his search for a Mexican wife.

Fifty-Two

Laurel and Larry offered us a place to park permanently on their tropical lands. Que bueno! A home for Jay to tend the trees of fruit and a paradise for me to sit and write. There was much to like about Todos Santos. Galleries, coffee shops with wi-fi and papaya ice cream. A small bookstore brimmed with handmade kitsch. Jay and I downed scrumptious fresh fish tacos at street stands for a buck fifty each. There was to-die-for carne asada (roasted/grilled beef) and pork tortas (grilled sandwiches on fresh bread rolls). We were living on $200-$300 a month and that had been one of our initial goals ... to live where we could survive on Jay's social security that would kick in the next year. Todos Santos, where the phone book was organized by first names.

Charming as it was, however, Todos was too gringo for my liking. Besides being a tourist magnet, the Americans who invested hundreds of thousands in upscale homes twisted an unsettling combo of spiritual chic and politic. Like the myriad of ex-pat communities I'd visited they accomplished many good deeds for the local peoples like clothing giveaways and school fundraisers. There was no end to good intentions. But with that came maneuvering and intense competition for a top-dog position I could only call gringo-jefe. In an uncanny turn of events, Americans came to Mexico and recreated the dramas they'd escaped in the USA.

"Todos Santos needs a gringa counselor, not to mention a mediator," Laurel said, tempting me. Therapy, Mexican style. We laughed as I envisioned myself going up and down the street with a Mexican machete, slicing and whacking away neuroses.

There it was, smack dab on our laps. Opportunity and invitation with two people we liked a *lot*. We could have stayed. We had no schedule or need to return, but something felt askew. Perhaps it was that pain in my neck. It could have been the landscape. Although the

Mexican mountains were stunning, I missed the lushness and wild of the Rockies, the scope of public lands on which to roam. Or maybe it was the idea of settling down, words that forced a rise of apprehension. The reason, no doubt, fell somewhere between a turkey, a moose and a family of whales—and hair that now reached my shoulders. The Baja birth canal had yet to deliver me.

Fifty-Three

Easter was a big concern as we rounded the Cape and began our Baja exit. It was Mexican ritual to pack up the family and *head for the beach*. We'd heard that one must be careful. If you were on a beach for the week of Easter break you wouldn't be able to come or go for so many people and cars. Already stressed and in pain, I voted to duck the crowds and stay at an RV park in Los Barriles (the barrels) on the east side of the Sea of California. Jay concurred.

We pulled into Martin Verdugo's Beach Resort and took a breath. They had a few spots left adjacent to the beach, along with a pool and a palapa bar that was run by crusty, old Mar-teen. It was also a popular windsurfing mecca, but by now the worst of the winter winds had subsided. Mostly it was American deep-sea fishermen and solo RV-women who had found themselves a chunk of nirvana. I was happy to park and not have to think about the road.

Well, sort of. We traded Tortuga for the Honda and took off to snorkel at Cabo Pulmo, a hidden, out of the way inlet a couple of hours south. We thought we'd beat the Easter rush. Not! The roads were straight out of *The Beverly Hillbillies*: mattresses, couches and chairs flopped over the backs of pickups and the tops of cars. Forget tie-downs; this was gravity packing and a prayer. I laughed out loud at the sight of trunks bulging with egg flats, coolers the size of coffins and mountains of potato chip bags. Giddiness filled the air in scenes of simple fun. Children and adults floated the gentle surf of the bay, played volleyball and soccer on the beach. We were a loooong way from our usual no-tan-line beach, but all was good as we hiked away from the hordes for the snorkel of our lives.

Warm, still waters combined with deep visibility and coral reefs to serve up outrageously colored, weird-bodied fish. Blue and yellow chromis, chameleon wrasse, Mexican hogfish, a sergeant major and stunning angelfish, spotted porcupine, Moorish idol, Mexican goatfish—it was one thrill and point after another. The gaudy waves of blue chin and bicolor parrotfish took the prize. Up to 2 ½ feet with parrot-like beaks, their pinks and rusts, neon blues and greens ruled the reefs. Baja had catapulted me into another reality once again.

Easter Sunday dawned with the call of church bells as Jay and I strolled across the village to Mass. Jay had done pretty well at finding churches for Sunday Mass with minimal inconvenience. At times my patience wore thin, however, as I wondered why he couldn't be like every other Catholic I knew and skip out once in awhile. In the early days of our relationship I went with him occasionally. I enjoyed the homilies and the "peace be with you," parts, but in the past few years I had gone less and less. The church's refusal to confront the sexual abuse of young boys was repulsive, and I grew tired of gravestones to the "unborn" outside church doors. I sided with the Indian elders I'd once sat with, who told me that no matter what white women might think, they couldn't kill souls.

The little church sat atop a hill at the end of a hundred uneven steps. Non-descript, almost ugly on the outside, we entered into a glistening, golden room. There were no Easter bunnies or bonnets. No baskets full of eggs and candy.

Dressed in a little pink sundress with dark brown ringlets, a little girl fidgeted by the organ where her diligent daddy sat and played as people entered the church. When it pleased her, she walked over and hit a few random high notes as her dad played on. Then, with an evil little grin, she turned and looked defiant at her mother, cringing next to us in the pew. Her mother waved her finger and sternly mouthed, *No!* whereupon the little munchkin pursed her lips, waved her finger and strongly nodded.

"She's going to be Pope someday," Jay whispered.

"Or president," I countered.

I initiated Lorena's pot that Sunday—cooked up the magic of La Candelaria in a soup of beef, garlic, and apples, almonds and green chiles. Then I threw in some raisins, oregano, cumin and lime. Caldo Ultimo!

Easter eve was our final night at Los Barriles. The gecko lizard that lived in the palm tree next to Tortuga began her periodic, scratchy chirp. I felt nostalgic as we toasted our final cape night.

Boats chugged into shore with their catches. A lone, snowy egret appeared on the beach to search for food at sundown. All was serene when suddenly on the horizon, as if on cue, manta rays burst straight up out of the water like kernels of popcorn. Hundreds of them, a hilarious, unbelievable sight.

According to one of the old fisherman, who took up his sunset roost at the al fresco bar, there were three theories: the rays jumped to get the barnacles off, they jumped to feed or they jumped for the hell of it. I figured it to have something to do with resurrection.

"Christina, stop!" Jay demanded. We were headed north. We'd just climbed that twisty, steep highway outside of Rosario, the strip that offered views down with no bottoms. Jay was dangerously close to the precipice and my body clenched every few minutes. I could hardly stand it and I couldn't get Jay to understand how close to the edge we were.

Dangerously close to the precipice, yes.

Fifty-Four

Rude awakenings take many forms. My body broke down. Dumped me like a load of rock in Cortez, Colorado. Not the winter's trendy stopover in Todos Santos, Baja Sur, where mangos hung heavy and Cuban Reds graced the banana bin. Not amidst Death Valley vertigo or the full moon rise under Delicate Arch. Nope, in non-descript Cortez, just a few miles up the road from the famous Four Corners tourist parking lot. That was where my body off-loaded me and forced a stop, just a few miles down the road from Mesa Verde, scene of that first devastating marriage meltdown.

We were parked in a friend's back yard when I rolled over in bed, prepared to lift out and meet the day, and pain as monstrous as labor shot down my arms. I got up, bent over and fell to the floor, writhing in a chaotic misfire of nerves. Then my writing hand index finger went numb.

Pain to stop me. Pain to scare the living hell out of me. I couldn't straighten my arms and put any weight on them. I couldn't move my stretched arms in a circular motion. No lifting. No washing. It hurt to walk on any surface that wasn't level. Movement, it seemed, was the metaphor. That night I had this dream:

Jay and I stood on the top, third floor balcony of a condo in the woods. (Three, holy trinity; top floors, the spiritual level.) We were happy and smiling. The feeling was carefree. I said to him, "Would we want the third floor?" I looked out at a mountain lion running across the stream. She had a brown tip on her tawny tail. I was thrilled by the sighting, when another lion and two brown bears also ran into view. The other lion's tail was lined in neon green. Then I noticed ribs. The group was emaciated and running for cover, *toward* the city. They disappeared into the trees as two Mexican men rushed up in a shiny SUV. They jumped from their car with walkie-talkies and radioed the animals' presence ahead in their effort to hunt them down.

My body faltered and forced a stop as the decimation of the earth and the wild came to me in a dream. I was in the midst of the most painful wake-up call of my life, desperate to regain some sense of center.

I changed my diet. The white flour and questionable oils of Mexico gave way to whole grains, fruits and olive oil. I bid farewell to sugary margaritas and alcohol and forced myself to walk every day. First one block, then two and more, the town grid became my lifeline as I walked and wondered whether all sickness wasn't homesickness.

My healers were many. One woman placed gemstones on my arms and shoulders to unlock the toxic energy. Carole conferred with me by phone and sent me a homeopathic remedy. Fascinating, it was phosphorous. As in lightning bugs and the metaphoric blinks of nerve mis*fires*.

I began a hefty regimen of herbal supplements and endured deep-tissue movement through Rolfing, as in, *ye-ouch!* the rolfer's hand reaching through my armpit and into my shoulder. A chiropractor showed me stretches and introduced me to the realization that in today's world the head is often tilted forward and down, a set-up for neck problems, which in turn, compressed the nerves. With his help I changed my posture and the position of my computer. My pillow was switched out for a rolled-up towel under my head.

My star healer, however, was Babette, who had recently opened a six-seater coffee shop on Main Street. I found her in my search for free wi-fi. Turned out she had been raised around Cortez and was one heck of a story teller. I loved her salty manner... the tales of motorcycle boyfriends, prison breaks and her insistence on the necessity to "cowgirl up," western-speak for face the music, stick to the program, do the work. We laughed out loud. A lot.

And therein was the secret. All of these things were raising my vibrational level and healing my body. I had heretofore seen reality as energy but hadn't made the scientific and spiritual connection that all energy carried a vibration. The higher the vibration, the better.

Gemstones, homeopathic remedies, walking and laughter were taking me home. My symptoms showed the *Way*.

I wondered whether my gypsy life had kinked the fuel line to my soul. I had absorbed the extremes of this life for over a year—the vibrant images, life-altering experiences and the ups and downs with Jay—but until this body breakdown had forced the issue, I hadn't sat still long enough to digest them. I had misjudged the responsibility that came with bearing witness, to transform what I was given through the pen. I wasn't stopped and out of gas. I was flooded. I could turn over but I couldn't get up and go.

Seemed my life was a Zen conundrum: I must sit still in order to move; I must move in order to sit still.

From my trip to the local library I'd ascertained my symptoms resembled those of fibromyalgia. From everything I read I was already doing everything that could be done. The only thing western medicine offered at that point were cortisone shots, and I wasn't about to do that. I finally got around to seeing my doctor after three months, once I had turned the malady around. He labeled my morass myofacial syndrome, a close cousin to fibro. He patted me on the head, said, "Good girl," and prescribed some heavy duty painkillers in case the pain returned. I rarely took even aspirin. I stashed the pills.

It took six months to change the fuel line and fill my tank with high octane. Jay continued work on his biography and applied to substitute teach in the local public schools as I emerged with a new dedication to my work. I redesigned my website, which had sat dormant for over a year. I said yes to a request to do a presentation for a monthly community group on the work of the soul and, most importantly, I wrote several hours a day, organizing notes from our travels and writing of our exploits. I was riding high about the prospect of a major writing project that would generate income. I'd sent Jay some drafts of my writing but I hadn't gotten them back, not even verbal comments. I asked him when I could expect them and he floored me with his response: he told me he wasn't going to read my writing any more. He was done.

We were writers, lovers, naturalists and adventurers, but above all, we were authors who supported one another in our writings. His declaration knocked the wind out of me. I went for a walk and sat down in the park with the Canadian geese. Then I got mad. As if picked up by an invisible force, I became more determined than ever to continue my dream. I ordered a screen house online to give me a separate writing space. I called it my Zen-den and it would travel wherever I went. My womb of one's own. From that day forward, I no longer wrote in concert with Jay. I wrote in spite of him.

The screen house arrived the same day I noticed an ad in the newspaper for "lab-mix" puppies. I called. "What's the mix?" I asked. The owner didn't know. He said Mama was a purebred yellow lab and dad was supposedly a purebred black lab but he wouldn't stake his life on it.

I drove the few miles out of town to the farmhouse where I narrowed six rambunctious pups down to two females. I removed the finalists from the pen to spend some time. I called them. I got down on all fours and wrestled with them. They were the sweetest little labs I'd ever seen. Eight weeks old, fat and spirited. One, however, was especially attentive. I tied a string around one pup's neck to reserve her until Jay could take a look. Jay met her the next day, and he was immediately smitten.

She had reddish highlights and golden patches behind her ears and down her neck. We named her Teak, since her coloring resembled the exotic wood. Sometimes she was Luna Teak (Lunatic) and sometimes she was Miss Teak (Mystic) but she was forever family. Pooka was not amused. She had moved into her spot as primo pet with gusto. Now she had to share attention, fun and games. Nose outta joint, she was miffed.

Miz Puppy Breath made me laugh. She pulled the focus away from myself just when I needed it. Teak took an instant liking to her kennel, which fit snugly beneath a pull-out table behind the passenger seat. She housetrained with few accidents. My computer adaptor was the first casualty. $35.00, ker ching. She was a free dog no more, and I hastily coiled and hid the electric cords.

Author partners (strike), lovers (strike), but still adventurers and naturalists, Jay and I set our sights on distant lands. We considered wintering in Big Bend National Park, then remembered that several months remained of our Mexican auto insurance. We lured ourselves with the prospect of a short drive into northern Mexico but my eye kept wandering down the map to a coastal town called Teacapán. It was perched on a huge estuary, which meant lots of birds, and it was below the Tropic of Cancer for warmth. It was about 70 miles south of Mazatlán off an easy four lane highway. In a huge shift from our itinerant life, we made plans to park there for the winter. I had learned to sit and stay as I taught the pup to sit and stay. Teak had reminded me that the first thing to do upon waking is to reach and stretch into the world.

Fifty-Five

Why did we keep to the road? Jay was grumbling, worried that money was getting low. He thought we should concentrate on income, but I believed that all would be well. I could not fathom giving up our life as writers. That's what we were to one another; it was the basis of our love. I believed the travel life was leading to *some*thing, and money would be attached to whatever that was. Bottom line, as long as we lived in Tortuga we were destined to migrate north and south with the change of seasons.

The travel south was blessedly easy, a wide toll road worth every expensive cent. Our only inland stop was Magdalena, where Padre Kino was buried. His tomb turned out to be a rather gruesome, exposed mass of bone and dirt, along the lines of the mummy museum I'd regretfully visited in Guanjuato several years before, and I had the same response: Get me out of here, before I throw up. The only extended stop was in Mazatlán to deliver a toothbrush.

I'd met Lynn online when I had inquired about Teacapán. She answered my posts about the area with detail and an impressive sense of experience. When I asked whether she needed anything from the U.S. she jumped at the chance to receive a special toothbrush. We arrived in Mazatlán just as the celebrations in honor of Our Lady of Guadalupe were gearing up. On December 12th we headed for the ancient Basilica in old Mazatlán in honor of her feast day and one of Mexico's largest fiestas.

Guadalupe's birthday was a long-standing tradition for me. I'd attended masses with Jay in Colorado and journeyed with girlfriends to Tortuga Mountain in Las Cruces, New Mexico, where I joined several hundred others in a reverent pilgrimage to the summit. Guadalupe was the dark-skinned Goddess of Mexico and mother to all Mexicans. I'd adopted her too, over the years, and had read every book about her I could get my hands on. Headed for the old Plaza of

Mazatlán, I was keyed up and totally unprepared for what I was about to see.

We entered the Basilica. It was brimming with statues and pictures of Our Lady. Vases of long-stemmed red roses and votive candles of every size and color covered the altar. The air was sweet with perfume. The pews were full, even though there was no Mass. Jay dropped to his knees in prayer as I took a seat. I stared up at the statue of Guadalupe until tears filled my eyes. I squeezed them shut and folded my hands in prayer. *Here I am*, I imparted. *Welcome me into your arms, Mi Madre.* I gave thanks for my life, rich in possibility, and my ever-improving health. I was 80% pain free, very much aware that many with fibromyalgia never return to such a vigorous state. I asked for blessings on my daughter, Hope. I followed that with turkey, moose and whale remembrances, and promised their visits wouldn't be in vain, wherever they led. The only thing I could think to ask for was grace, the faith to believe the road I was on was true.

We rose and made our way toward the door. In front of me, in the slow-moving line, was a mother holding her brown-eyed baby boy. His thick lashes slowly opened and closed as he peered over her shoulder at me. I smiled and instantly did a double take as I saw a black mustache painted above his lip. I gazed around me to see *all* little boys under the age of three were dressed as little Juan Diegos, the peasant man to whom Our Lady of Guadalupe first appeared in the mountains.

The story goes that She presented Juan with fresh roses in the middle of December in order for him to prove her existence to the church officials. Every boy wore white cotton peasant clothes and donned Juan mustaches, a comical, heart-rending scene!

The little girls, on the other hand, wore red kerchiefs on their heads and strutted proudly in their multicolored peasant skirts. On their backs, positioned between their shoulder blades, hung intriguing little cages about ten inches wide and eight inches tall. Later that day, in the packed, bustling market, I saw these cages for sale, bought one and hung it inside of Tortuga. When Lynn arrived to pick up her toothbrush the small cage caught her attention. She phoned her Mexican neighbor who told her the cage was called a *java* (pronounced hă-ba). It replicated the items one carried for spiritual pilgrimage.

Indeed, affixed to the little wood and wire crate were miniature replicas of necessities for a sacred journey: a sombrero to protect one from the sun, a tortilla press, a clay water jug, a straw basket and a lava stone *molcajete* in which to cook stews over a fire. A plate and various pieces of cookware dangled from the bottom. A rolled-up lime-green sleeping mat stretched across the top. A turquoise and pink striped serape adorned the side, next to a tiny picture of—who else?—Our Lady.

The java was a symbol of one who rids herself of possessions and embarks on a spiritual pilgrimage. I mused that the articles represented weren't that different from the few things I chose to carry in the motorhome. Just the basics. To top it off, the door on the back of the little cage was open: loose chickens!

We departed Mazatlán through a stunning sea of red. The Christmas poinsettias had arrived from a multitude of Mexican greenhouses. Parking lots and streets were lined in scarlet plants, from eight inches small to rotund bushes. I bought two red and one white for our holiday centerpiece, which would eventually take up the entire dashboard space inside Tortuga's windshield.

Eighty southbound miles delivered us to Teacapán. We opted to stay a few miles out of town, choosing the open Pacific over Teacapán's protected estuary. The Villas Onac was simple and quiet—a few little casitas, a gorgeous tiled pool and a line of 20-some RV spaces that faced crashing ocean waves. Jay began every day at water's edge in his morning meditation. I walked the endless, undeveloped beach, high tide and low. Somewhere along the playa I stopped to do a short regimen of stretches. A combination of pilates, yoga and high school gym class. Once back to Tortuga I finished up on the floor. I was amazed at how little attention the body actually needed to stay healthy. Fifteen minutes of focused movement a day and a good walk.

Dusty little Teacapán was replete with a run-down plaza, a little Catholic church and a window where people lined up to buy their morning tortillas. I stood transfixed as I watched the hand-mixed dough dumped into a bin. A wide, tattered belt moved the machine-shaped tortillas through heat and into the hands of a teenage girl with thick blue eye shadow and mascara to match. She wore tight, low-cut jeans, as she stacked the golden rounds into high, warm piles.

The line was long to buy corn tortillas and no doubt longer in order to watch the girls. Clever business strategy! A kilo of tortillas cost a few pesos, about fifty cents.

It was too windy to put up the screen house on the beach. While contemplating complicated solutions for a separate writing space I awakened one morning with the idea of a bungee cord strung across Tortuga with a piece of fabric draped over. The next day I found Teacapán's little hardware store and searched for a cord. In the midst of shelves of organized chaos I came across a roll of orange plastic, small-link chain. Two small 'S' hooks, a package of clothespins and I was good to go. What fun. The clothespins were funky-weird wire little things. I reckoned they were peyote-button inspired.

I lifted the bed and pulled a piece of fabric from storage... a gorgeous fuchsia print of vibrant gold fish, teal flowers and patterned fans. Carole had brought it from China. Mission accomplished! My muse danced within my separate little space. I wrote and, sadly, reviewed my words in isolation. I sorely missed my writing partner.

As on the Baja, we were surrounded by Canadians, bookended by Vancouver Island and Calgary. Alan, Donna, and Ted the cat were to our right. Magicians of stone, they fashioned stunning pieces of jewelry from rock they found and polished. Wally and Dolly pulled in on our left, commandeering an aged, renovated city bus. Jovial folks with three yippy dogs and a hankering for fun, they were our leads to special restaurants and excursions into the mountains to east. Wally also spent several days helping Jay rig a replacement stop valve on the water heater.

When we tired of cooking or just wanted a party we headed for Teacapán and our favorite little outdoor restaurant on the beach. Alex-the-waiter brought by a cooler and we chose our dinner from the day's catch—scallops, white fish, shrimp—and minutes later it appeared in front of us with salsas, salads and warm corn tortillas. Con cervezas y margaritas, sí!

We built a large bonfire on Solstice Eve, compliments of driftwood collected on many beach walks. Teak at our feet, we sat with friends as the sun eased into the sea. The longest night was upon us and I took serious comfort in my blessings. It had taken two years but Jay and I had finally found the rhythm that worked for a life on wheels. We now stopped for several months at a time and practiced the art of interlude. But our relationship had taken dramatic shifts. On this longest night I wasn't sure what I wanted to shed in my life—or perhaps more importantly, what I wanted to keep.

Days flowed by. I wrote and walked and let the rhythms of the sea possess me. My favorite dinner became fresh, hot popcorn with nutritional yeast sprinkled on top. Yellow flakes across the floor, yellow flakes on the couch and yellow flakes in the bed. I siesta'd after lunch, read the final tome of *The Dark Materials Trilogy*.

We hadn't known that sea turtles were our neighbors. We celebrated their mysterious tracks as they emerged from their watery homes, struggled on squat legs up steep dunes beyond the high-tide line, dug a hole and laid their eggs. These ancient symbols of eternal life clawed ferociously, pushing sand over eggs, before risking hours of detection on the open beach until low-tide signaled *go*.

It was mid-day when Jay and I came upon a female. We watched as she slowly, deliberately crawled into the salty sea only to be picked up by waves and pounded back to shore. She entered again. Returned. After several more tries she disappeared into the sunless depths, completing the ritual of 150 million years, her meeting with the moon and the endless cycle of the wild.

Oneiric days followed one after another. I lost myself in the gentle waves of tide, the patterns of sea foam on the beach. A lacey piece of fishing net of twine and shell washed to shore; a seal, pecked eyeless, laid supine on the beach, vultures in wait. And then one day, bees dead at water's edge. Soggy wings, minute legs bare of pollen sacs. From that day forward I saw them every morning.

Solemn scenes and Teak at play. She learned to swim in the forceful waves, diving straight-on and holding her head above the salty crests. Fetch dog extraordinaire, her favorite toy was a plastic bottle, half-filled with water or sand, so it lofted far and floated upright, visible in the waves. She was a wonder to watch, a constant rhythm of throw-go-and-get.

I meandered along the endless sand on Christmas Eve, a meditation of swaying palm and soggy footprints in the sand. Teak raced ahead, nose to the ground, scouring the beach for a coconut to fetch. A hefty wave curled and broke. Six, seven more lined up behind it on their way to meet the shore in a hypnotic advance of foam.

Three dolphins appeared thirty feet off shore and kept time with my stride. Two adults and one babe dove and surfaced, the western sun glancing off their gleaming, gray skin. They accompanied me for over a mile, diving and surfacing in a miraculous interplay of spirit. I flashed on memories of aboriginal Australian cave paintings: depictions of tiny people-bubbles birthed from dolphin blowholes.

A wave, exceeding all others, swelled and strengthened upon the sea. The sunlight shot through the back of its roll. It peaked and broke in a deluge of white foam. For one glorious moment the three dolphins appeared inside the wave—vertical fins, bottlenose snouts, within a diaphanous womb.

You asked for grace, Christina. We'll give you grace.

Fifty-Six

The full moon grabbed my womb and impelled her to bleed again. After many months of empty and "I'm sure I'm done with that," she yanked my body... back? forward?... Once again the menstruating woman, conduit of moon, earth and sea. And, I welcomed the familiar warmth of an old friend coming back for one more visit.

I had never been more present than when the womb let go in a rush of blood. My place on the earth was wrapped within that fall from non-linear realms, and now I read that dolphins knew when a woman menstruates. *Dolphin*, from the Greek word *delphinos,* which meant *womb*.

The convergence was uncanny. First, a dolphin family walking me along the beach, leading me to a finale that struck to my core, then the pull of my womb and release of blood. One can not witness such a scene and walk away with merely, "Wasn't that cool?" No, this was another level of synchronicity.

Climate change, hardly a whisper when we'd started this odyssey, was now on the public radar; and along with that, the monumental role of oceans in earth's survival. Air and water had danced for eons in a free exchange of balance. Gases from the air were gulped by the sea, dissolved and returned to the air in a dance of equal parts. Shockingly, since the industrial age, half the CO_2 that humans produced has stayed in the oceans. The pH of the oceans wavers as seas turns to acid.

Every day, every American added forty pounds of carbon dioxide to the seas.

Even if emissions stopped tomorrow, it would take over 10,000 years to remedy. Were it not for the seas, say the scientists, the CO_2 would stay in the air and great disaster would befall us. The dolphins and whales, oh yes, they knew their home would roil and burn.

Fifty-Seven

I emailed our mail delivery service our forwarding address: General Delivery, Patagonia, Arizona. Winter on the Mexican Pacific had been sublime. My body had healed, we'd made good friends and it was not easy to leave. Now five months old, Teak hurdled the closest wave and swam against the building surf to fetch a floating coconut. Instinct bound, I could not teach her the ways of the retriever. She taught me—to head out against the surge, keep the eye on the prize, time the catch, paddle the turn and ride the waves of the incoming surf back to shore.

To follow my instinct and bring it home.

Tortuga swayed side to side down the sandy lane that led to the highway. I said a silent adios to my morning walk through the bushy green chile plants as I wondered whether these fields were the genesis of the dead bees. A teenage Mexican boy walked with long strides down the long rows, a plastic tank of insecticide on his back. He was dressed in a black t-shirt and faded jeans. A metal chain drooped around his neck. Cheap vinyl sneakers covered his feet and his head was bare. Up a row, down a row, up and down. He held the thin metal nozzle over the blooming plants. No bandana covered his mouth and nose to stop the breeze-blown spray from reaching his lungs.

A diminutive campesino walked the opposite field. The old man wore a long-sleeved white shirt and weathered sandals. A kerchief over his mouth, he had donned a sombrero cut from a stained cardboard box. His steps were quick and short as he sprayed the deadly mist.

We all breathe together, I thought as I took a page from Thich Nat Hanh. I was the young, cool Mexican boy who showed up to work and collected his few pesos a day. I was the old man hunched over a meal of tortillas and beans, who prayed to Guadalupe for another day of... grace.

We turned onto the highway and accelerated toward our slow and steady 55 mph. *Thump. Thump. Thump.* Soft, sickening thuds hit the windshield smearing small swaths of yellow across the glass. Thump. Bees. Thousands swarmed across the road into the path of traffic. I looked down as I covered my ears.

Fifty-Eight

It was good to be back in the USA where every grocery sold Half & Half and I didn't have to worry that an accidental swallow of tap water would turn my gut inside out. My first meal was a juicy mesquite-grilled hamburger with crunchy fries. My first purchase was a toaster. Alas, not the $60.00 sexy red one I'd seen months ago in Durango. I opted for a $6.00 one in boring white that would live in the cupboard next to Jay's granola. The toaster came in, the tea kettle went out. There were many ways to boil water. The tea kettle had never justified the space it consumed. One thing in, one thing out.

The odometer on Tortuga turned over to 34,000 miles as we pushed across the border in Nogales. We had bought her two years ago with 14,000. Twenty thousand miles in two years. Twenty thousand miles and how many lifetimes? I remember our delightful French friends on Scammon's Lagoon who remarked that you need one lifetime just for Paris.

It was 22 degrees in Naco, Arizona, on March 1st. The water froze in the hose so I pressed a button and switched over to the internal water supply to fulfill the duties of the morning: flushed the toilet, brushed my teeth and made coffee. I switched the heat from quiet propane to the noisier electric furnace. All was well in self-contained Tortuga-land as I pulled the handle of the shower faucet, stepped into the sky-lit stall and sang the praises of hot water. Blessed be.

Pooka's golden tipped pelt caught the sun's first rays on the dashboard and Teak awaited her morning walk patiently from within her kennel. Jay was in the bedroom reading his morning meditation as I sorted through our monthly box of mail. Four more *New Yorker*s. Last month's *AARP Magazine*. A postcard from my cousin

Georgia. The Border Patrol helicopter made its first pass, scanning the landscape for last night's border breachers.

The U.S. news was full of David Bradshaw and his 100 million bees that had gone missing. He joined beekeepers in twenty-four states with empty hive boxes. The strange thing was there were no bee bodies on the ground outside the hives where bees normally discarded their dead. The empty colonies were full of honey, pollen and larvae, in an eerie disappearance.

"Colony collapse disorder," said the scientists as sound bites flowed like warm honey. More than 90 different fruits, veggies and seeds were pollinated by the fluttering visits of bees. One third of our diet. The healthiest part. I flashed back to the soggy bees of Mexico that had lost their homing device.

No one knew how many bees were in this country so no one knew how many had disappeared. No one seemed to care as long as they pollinated and plants bore fruit. In ancient cultures, however, bees were sacred. The bodies of the dead were preserved in honey and bees were a symbol of resurrection. Bees' wax was turned to candles. The hexagon of the honeycomb was considered an expression of Aphrodite's spirit. Pythagoreans, meanwhile, reflected on the honeycomb's continuous sixty-degree triangular lattice, a hexagonal miracle considered to be the underlying symmetry of the cosmos.

It was once believed that if bees abandoned their hive it was a sign that the beekeeper would soon die. I was beginning to think that the death of the beekeeper was just the beginning.

Fifty-Nine

Arizona's heat resumed her familiar role of spoiler and pushed us north into Colorado. Gas prices were edging near $3.00 a gallon and our stocks weren't doing as well as we'd hoped. Even our "safe" investments were taking dives. So far we'd done okay with Jay's seasonal, substitute teaching and our freelance articles, but events of the world definitely were shifting.

We landed in Mancos to house sit, once more in the shadow of Mesa Verde. We took care of a friend's house for a month, long enough for me to get to know and like the small town whose motto was, *Where the West Still Lives!* Mancos, population around 800, was positioned in one of the most beautiful valleys on earth. Problem was, a 4-lane highway lined with chain-link fence split the town in half. It was ugly to passersby and made it difficult to gain entrance. Find your way into its downtown main street, however, and there was a café/bakery that brimmed with community chatter. A little wildlands park became a favorite of Teak's, the goal of our daily walk and her afternoon dive into current to fetch a stick. Non-sexy Mancos was small, simple and easy.

Our month drew to a close as I knocked on John's door. I'd been admiring the whimsical renovation he had worked on his old farmhouse and it was high time I stopped to tell him so. His blue eyes twinkled as he opened the door. Knee pads and a torn flannel shirt were the perfect accompaniment to his unruly gray hair. We chatted a bit and when I told him we were packing up to move he declared, "Nope!" He picked up his cell phone and called Betsy, who owned the empty lot next to him at the end of the gravel road. Just like that we had a beautiful place to park on land by the Mancos River. We hooked up to John's electricity and water.

I set up the Zen-den near water's edge and wrote every day. Jay began to network and check out possibilities of environmental consulting. About this time we had an email from the buyer of our house in Taos. He wondered whether we wanted to return and take care of the property while he underwent treatment for a brain tumor. He even offered to put in a pad and hookups for Tortuga.

A return to Taos didn't interest us but I was amazed at yet another invitation to settle down. Naco, Cortez, Todos Santos and now Taos. It was somehow reassuring; it made me confident that yes, options were floating around out there. But no way did I picture myself settled down in one spot long-term. Old chunks of my life were falling away, but as long as wonders never ceased I was along for the ride. We made plans to head for British Columbia. Carole and Chris had traded the Boulder fast lane for a wild piece of land up north. The way gas prices were acting we figured we'd best hit the road.

Then Jay was blindsided by West Nile Virus while sitting along the Mancos River.

He went flat: no life force, no energy and an axe-splitting headache. Doc said there wasn't anything he could do. Jay had to ride it out and one day he'd wake up feeling normal again. P.S. In three to six months.

After three weeks in bed Jay decided if he was going to feel like the living dead he'd just as soon be with friends in BC. The stock market had spiked a bit and delivered some unexpected greenbacks. Off we headed, slow and easy. As we hit the highway there was a crazy-sounding scream. Our heads snapped as we looked at one another, "What the hell?" Then James Brown erupted into his classic tune, "I feel good..." It was the Mother's Day card that Hope had sent me, programmed to burst out in song when it was opened. I cracked up. Jay wasn't amused.

Sixty

I was eager to see Carole. She and Chris had been in Canada only a few months, leaving behind life in the US for a chance to live their dream and create an organic farm at the edge of wilderness. Carole met us at the bottom of their driveway and led us up the drive, where we settled on their land in between two creeks amidst emerald-green fern, cedar, and hemlock. The Purcell Wilderness rose steep to the east across Kootenay Lake. Morning began with her sun-sliced cleavage and slowly evolved into dramatic light shows of cliff, glacier and forest.

We were now in the land of twilight where light lingered until after ten p.m. and etched the sky at 3:00 a.m., when birds awoke in song and the lake turned rose with dawn. It reminded me of Denmark. Thank the goddess for room-darkening shades.

Our life on the side of the mountain was a collage of group and solo adventures, topped off with homegrown meals and wine. The four of us kayaked across the lake to a deserted beach. Not your normal little watering hole, the Kootenay ranged anywhere from two to five miles wide and was a hundred miles long. She made her own weather and demanded attention to detail.

Canadian wilderness was a different world from wilderness south of the border. Steep canyon hikes delivered us to rushing, blue-green glacier water and foam. Exhilaration and death were constant partners. There were no babbling brooks in the Purcells. This was the land of wild force. And everywhere was grizzly land. Hikes were never relaxed jaunts to a scenic vista. Trails were strewn with warm piles of grass-laden scat about the size of a cow pie. We learned humility fast and sang really loud around blind corners. While Mexico had demanded one kind of intense awareness, these lands demanded another, equally intense.

The hiking days of nerve-wracking elation required down time. Jay's energy came in short bursts. He sank into Cormac McCarthy's, *The Road* one day and energetically weed-whacked ferns that threatened to take over every inch of pasture land the next. He accompanied Carole and Chris on cherry-picking expeditions but regretfully declined an opportunity to backpack for several days with Chris into the alpine. I'd never seen him refuse an offer like that. West Nile had him by the gonads.

Pooka Java Gem ran free. Teak swam. I retreated every morning to my Zen-den which I'd tucked between two towering cedars on a spot where the creek submerged. Amidst whisking, furling energies I wrote as I sipped *Grizzly Claw—dark roasted with bold attitude*. Another coffee bean label to add to my collection.

Only four days remained before our departure. I pushed to hike the Alps Alturas trail, captured by guidebook descriptions of the high mountain tundra and breathtaking alpine meadows. Hyped and raring to go, the four of us made plans for the farewell hike. It was steep but only about eight miles long, so Jay thought he could do it.

The next morning we miraculously convened *on time* in the kitchen at 6:00 a.m. Chris plied us with blueberry pancakes he made from scratch as we downed strong coffee. Lunches packed, dogs and gear in the back of the pickup, we set off. The weather couldn't have been more perfect.

It was a lengthy, steep mountain drive on dirt to the trailhead. Jay and I had learned to, shall I say, *appreciate* trailheads in British Columbia. In barely three weeks we'd been turned away from hiking attempts by heli-log closures, landslides, floods, fallen trees, overgrowth and a crazy woman who had put up an electric fence and blocked access to three major drainages. We only made it to our destination trailhead about 50% of the time. So far this day had unfolded like a perfectly choreographed play.

The hike began through sub-alpine forest and opened up on high glacier meadows surrounded by craggy, steep cliffs. Jay, Carole and I took our time under heaving cumulous clouds as Chris ventured ahead. Yellow columbine and bulging purple penstemon peppered the grasses. Mountain heather and fuzzy, long-stemmed anemones jiggled in the breeze. Up, up we climbed, along streamside and beds of rose.

"Oh, I can relax now," Carole said. "There aren't any bears this high."

I arched my eyebrows at her false sense of security. The higher Jay and I had trekked last week the more hair we saw in the bear scat; the lower we were, the more berries. Now we had just passed a long line of deep holes where great claws had excavated the chambers of underground pika and marmots. Impressive and humbling, it got my attention.

We stopped for a snack with a view of snow-laden peaks beyond. On top of the world. Above timberline... I relished the expanse; the spine-tingling air, the utter feel of vulnerability. I walked to a higher viewpoint, signaling Jay to join me for a romantic moment, but he didn't. The next thing I knew he was walking on with nary a call or goodbye. Chris, the only one with pepper spray, had taken off ahead and was out of sight. In short, we were doing exactly what all experts say not to do in grizzly country: hike spread out and separate.

I trotted to catch up with Carole. We had gone about two miles when Carole and I came around a bend to face Chris' wide eyes and an extended, flattened palm, signaling stop. He gestured *shush* and then pointed below. I leashed the dog and joined him. "Grizzly," he whispered.

Just thirty yards below were a sow and two cubs. Exhilaration and gut-wrenching fear shot through me like an electric shock. Jay rounded the corner as I signaled the bear's presence to him. We were thankfully downwind but what would Mama Griz do when she finally saw us? I had seen bears make their way up mountainsides in split-second runs, and we were above tree line with no cover. I watched Mother's every move, sending *We're not here to harm you* vibes.

I drank in the scene for a couple of minutes. The browsing bears were not rotund and glossy. They bordered on emaciated. Like the lions and bears in my distant dream, some ribs showed through their coats. They had a lot of eating to do before winter set in; I preferred not to be on the menu. Suddenly, one of the yearlings looked up at us. The moment of truth. Mama Griz glanced at her cubs and then stared at us again for several seconds. My breath stopped. As if on cue, her brood moved to her side and followed her down the mountain into the cover of krumholz.

Exhale! I was ecstatic in the wake of the sighting. I couldn't stop grinning as Carole said, "Let's go back! We've seen them. Let's go."

There was no way I was moving off that mountain out of bear's energy field. I was witness to a wonder, fervently alive and in the moment. After several minutes the three bears appeared on an adjacent slope, grazing their way up the mountainside. This time I reached for the camera.

"We've got to go," Carole insisted. "See? They're circling around. They're going to cut us off. Oh my God, they're going to block our way out!"

Carole was scared to death; I was scared to life. We discussed continuing to the end of the trail but Carole was having none of it.

"I'm going back," she said.

"Well, go back then," Chris said.

I looked from Carole to Chris and across to the bears and rendered my own assessment. Momma grizzly had not looked for confrontation. She had sought to avoid. I glassed as she led the cubs and continued to forage, flipping over small boulders in search of insects as if they were pieces of gravel. Awash in bliss and adrenaline I wanted to continue on and find a place sit and decompress. I looked at Carole. "Just a little ways farther?"

Jay nodded. Chris was already a few steps up the trail as Carole gave up and came along.

We were rewarded with an open mountainside of soft, emerald tundra. Spiderweb waterfalls traced their way down mountain cliffs to a turquoise lake. The four of us fell into separate silences as we put down our packs and took a breath, a mix of elation and hyper-alert. I sat near Jay; we were together, yet eerily apart.

Our return to the truck was a timeless blur. The four of us mixed gravity with laughter as we sang our way down the mountain and out of the fear. Strange how the psyche responds to get you over the hump. "If you go down to the woods today you're sure of big surprise," sprang from my lips. "If you go down to the woods today you'd better go in disguise." I hadn't sung "Teddy Bear Picnic" since I was eight!

I don't recall a pickup ever looking so good. We heaved sighs of relief as four arms reached simultaneously into the cooler and we each pulled out a cold, dark beer. Toast: glad to be alive! *Klunk.*

Mostly we stood around like zombies in a semi-comatose state as our bodies sought some semblance of normalcy.

Sixty-One

I retreated to the Zen-den the next morning, fountain pen and journal in hand. The stream tumbled down the hill at my side through a rotten stump and under the moss-covered ground. A pileated woodpecker's gaping hole stared out at me from a cedar's elegant side. There was comfort in his unmistakable excavation, three inches high and an inch wide. And today, post-griz, I would take what comfort I found.

The shadows of feathery hemlock swayed trancelike upon the screen; a bumble bee flew in one door, zinged past my head, and buzzed out the other. As if on cue I began to tremble and tears burst forth. The seal of terror broke in the wake of the golden sow's sheer size and power. Her command of the yearlings who grazed at her side. Her ultimate reign over the landscape. The holy fright and awe.

Nature had just upped the ante. Turkey, moose, whale, dolphin—my contact with them was about eye contact and connection, a potent transfer of energy. This top-of-the-food-chain encounter was different. My soul shuddered. I was poignantly aware of second chances.

I lay back in my lounge chair and closed my eyes, giving way to sleep. I dreamed I was launched on a bike into the air, flying like an airplane on pedal power, a glorious scene! I awoke with the strong urge to launch, to join monarch butterflies and Canadian geese and begin the migration south. Jay had committed to a semester-long teaching job near Mancos, filling in for a teacher on pregnancy leave. I, on the other hand, needed to be in one place to regurgitate the implausible past events, to pull taut the threads of my life.

I scanned my altar and reached into the Papago Indian basket that held the stones I had collected from many years; ones that had called to me along the way. Among them was the one and only crystal I had ever dug from the ground over 20 years ago. I approached the cedar tree and her pileated woodpecker hole and squeezed the crystal into the oblong excavation. Then I turned, blew out the candle and walked away.

Perhaps someone someday would find it, as I had found the one embedded in Grandmother Tree's ponderosa bark so many moons ago, that time when dreams foretold and omens pushed, when Grandmother had counseled that I could not chase what was meant to be... and to grow my hair long.

Tortuga's engine started right up after her month's rest at Two Creeks, the name I had given to Chris and Carole's home. Every breath taken on their land, every gesture born, every drink swallowed took place between the two creeks that served as their boundaries, north and south. Chris plied us with the morning's eggs and a sack full of fresh garden bounty. We departed as we had arrived, on the full moon.

Jay made his way slowly down the hill from Two Creeks to the highway. I followed in the car, watching Tortuga gently rock back and forth as tears welled in my eyes. "That's my *house*," I whispered. "My *house*... rolling down the road toward her next phenomenal resting place." I was suddenly struck by an image of me driving off alone, waving goodbye as I left Jay in the dust.

Sixty-Two

We bypassed Mancos and parked at the edge of a pond in a place called Boggy Draw. Surrounded by Ponderosa, Spruce and Aspen at 9,000 foot elevation, we were twenty miles from the school where Jay was teaching. He departed every morning around 7:00, leaving me to Autumn's solace. I was devoted to the written word, determined to frame the staggering past three years. I could feel the collage beginning to gel but I couldn't yet get the picture. There were the encounters with the wild that spoke to something larger than me, and there were the increasing disappointments in my marriage. But beyond those threads lurked something larger. When I stopped and slowed down I filled with a mixture of curiosity and anxiety; I was on a one-way road to a reckoning, I reckoned. I could bail or I could ride it out. Avoidance never was my forte.

Teak slept curled at my feet as I coaxed last night's campfire to flame and warmed my toes against the morning's frosty air. Peach pie breakfast lingered on my lips as book pages turned ghostlike in the breeze. Attempts to write were quelled by Pooka, who took up residence on my belly. The Bengal kneaded away as if it were a bowl of dough. It was comforting until the point where she got carried away and included her claws. *Enough!* I thought as we jumped in unison from the chair.

I grabbed my binoculars and took to the forest in search of surprise. It might be a bird but could just as easily be a butterfly, an animal track in mud or a glimpse of a fleeing black bear. I, at home in the nomad's life, far afield from sluggish routine. Loose woman, flirt of the forest. Flirt, as in short flights of birds. Loose, as in free. Not confined.

I, positioned to witness, that I might tell you how a feather falls from sky. How it floats upright, twirls and swirls a free-fall down, spins and points her quill into Mother Earth.

Part III

No Apologies

Sixty-Three

We perused the map, looking for a Thanksgiving week venture. The Valley of the Gods looked like the ticket. Ringed by a lonely dirt road about twenty miles west of Bluff, Utah, it was far from a major population center, had just one access road, no power lines and was out of cell phone range. Perfect! One of those places that was on the way to someplace else. It didn't hold the sex appeal, tours and gift shops of its larger sister forty miles down the road, Monument Valley.

Jay turned Tortuga down a hill; we rocked back and forth across an arroyo as we headed into massive spires of red rock. Once more in boondock heaven, my plan was to write and photograph, create an article for a Durango magazine. Jay and I spent the first two days hiking up sandy washes into deep canyonlands. Afternoons drenched us in hot sun as short days quickened our steps. We'd return to Tortuga salty with sweat, brimming with satisfied tiredness. The best!

November's Beaver Moon waxed toward full, draping sandstone pinnacles in phantom light. We'd completed dinner and were having another glass of wine in the red glow of sundown, the perfect end to the full day. I walked over to Jay, nuzzled my face against his and gave him a peck on the lips. I was exhausted and ready to hit the sack. Jay followed and began to push for more. I responded with, "Oh Babe, how about we just lie together and cuddle? I'm beat."

It was the status quo these days, a huge imbalance in our needs and desires. He pushed for sex every night. I was desperate to escape the pressure pot, had recently suggested a compromise of sex every 3 or 4 days. And then we argued over whether it was day 3 or day 4. This is when you know you've hit the dregs in the bottom of the coffee mug. Jay defaulted to his M.O., silent anger, and for the second time in our twelve-year marriage he took off in the car with nary a word.

Oh great. I was at the end of my rope, like that collie in the dream, hanging, swaying but still alive. I tossed every bottle of alcohol outside and emptied them onto the ground. I screamed to the moon and the coyote answered. I was done with sex on demand. *Talk to me, Jay. Talk to me, damn it!* It was the most popular phrase in my journal.

Pooka curled nervously at my side as I stared at the bedroom mirror where I had affixed favorite photos from my life as we began the full-time journey. I'd unintentionally created a collage of my life. Me standing on a hillside in my hippie garb, pregnant with Hope. Aunt Clara in a flowery sack dress amidst her siblings dressed in gray; Inga at the mailbox on the gravel road, her favorite goose at her feet; Jay's photo id from his 1968 Berkeley days; Fyre, my Arabian horse, prancing high and proud; Jay on one knee, surrounded by gaudy artificial flowers, proposing for our renewal vows at the Hitching Post Chapel in Las Vegas; my dapper Dad standing with his arms wrapped around my feisty teenaged Mom; Hope sitting lazily by the woodstove in my cabin, writing, a contented cat on her lap. My gaze landed on the photo of the altar I had created in the jungle of Tikal before I saw a jaguar, one of the most empowering moments of my life.

I rose from the bed and approached the sliding door where I'd taped a page from the Sunday New York Times several months before. The page was blank except for the words in the middle: *Imagine living life in peace.* It was signed Yoko Ono, her New Years message to the world. I inserted an arrow between *imagine* and *living* and scribbled the words, *Jay and Christina.*

Camera and binocs around my neck, I stepped outside to shoot dawn's light on sandstone spires. I was free. I moved across the red soils, alone and vibrant, snapping pictures. The Navajo perceive the weather-sculpted rock as warriors frozen in time, whom they call upon for protection. Carved by water, wind and erosion for 250-million years, the power of the place cast a wholly different energy for me. I fell in love with that lusciously lonesome place, waiting for the light to be just right, snapping pictures and writing. I was dwarfed by the immensity of pinnacles, vast sky and pounding quiet, and they loomed as sisters of mercy.

Night fell early, leaving me to myriad thoughts, questions and bottomless exasperation. There I was, nudging sixty, with no steady income or health insurance and a body that had sagged into various gelatinous directions. We had our problems, yes, but didn't all relationships go through rocky years? Now I wondered whether that was the right question. I'd lived one quarter of my life with Jay. After that amount of time you not only live *with* someone, you live *through* him. Relationships—everyone makes their deals.

I set up my camera and stood before it, taking pictures of my body, which had put on a few extra pounds. I was determined to shed the extra weight, take the metaphor as far as needed.

I was dialing in the weather channel on the radio when I picked up word of the first snowstorm of the season. I had 24 hours to hit the road; less if I wanted to be somewhere safe and sound. There was no cell service and little chance of exit should I get snowed in. I packed up camp, attending first to the inside of Tortuga. Then I moved to Jay's half, the outside, folding chairs, putting away the grill, rolling the rug, stretching my mind to remember the details as the wind roared around me. *Damn you! Where are you, Jay?*

Pooka leapt into the passenger chair as I turned the key. I pressed my foot on Tortuga's broad gas pedal, and as she crawled forward the Honda came into view. I heaved a sigh of relief as we met in the wind with an embrace of habit. He said he'd gone to Denver to see his mother. There was no apology, but it didn't matter. Something had shifted in me out there under Venus. My soul had forged a deep bond with wild space, as the inertia of marriage waned amidst coyote's feral howl.

We returned to our parking spot on the Mancos River while Jay completed his teaching semester. I took to building morning fires and sitting in the frigid air. My hair crept below my shoulders.

Sixty-Four

Despite months beyond spring and summer runoff, the McElmo River still had an edge. The current was formidable enough that we had to carefully select where to cross. We were with a good friend on our way to some petroglyph panels. The barren hillside walks weren't long, but the day was frigid and windy. We came across some vibrant Kokopellis etched upon the blackened sandstone boulders that had separated and fallen from the ruddy mesa cliffs above. Their brilliance warmed the core.

We considered heading home after three hours but decided on one more jaunt to a rock monolith. A gradual climb up a hill and a zigzag through rock boulders delivered us to remarkable horizontal line of animals, people and spiral designs etched into the rock. The line was about fifteen feet long: an ancient calendar. We sat in a sunny spot out of the wind and gazed at the detail before us. What a miraculous drawing. How blessed was I, to land in that sacred, ancient place of power.

The solstice sun cast faint, long shadows as we headed for the car around 3 p.m. It would set within an hour and I was reeling from the day of riches. Midway to the car I looked down to see the strangest looking rock I'd ever spied. I picked it up for close examination. It was smooth to my skin, in stark contrast to the drab sandy dirt and dark rock that surrounded it. The oval wonder filled the palm of my hand and had the heft of what I'd expect of a very hard rock that size. And it looked as if it had just jumped out of some rock hound's polishing machine.

"A gastrolith!" exclaimed my friend, an ardent armchair archeologist. Carol. *Gastro*, as in *stomach*; *lith*, as in *stone*. Aka, *gizzard stone*. The fist-sized wonder came from the insides of a dinosaur that had swallowed it to aid in digestion. I felt as if I'd stumbled across the Holy Grail, made even more improbable by the fact that I rarely find things on the ground. I'm a birder; I look up. But there weren't any trees on these empty lands. Just rock and dirt and a grey-brown gizzard stone.

I reckoned the gastrolith came from something like an Armored Stegosaurus, a bus-sized herbivore with small teeth who browsed on the mosses, ferns, conifers and fruits that once covered those desert lands, a tropical, cycad-covered landscape of 155 million years ago. She had two rows of tall spikes upon her back, thus her name that translated as "roof lizard." She walked on two or four legs and grew to 14 feet tall and 30 feet long. And she swallowed rocks.

It was easy to forget that the arid lands around me were once Jurassic Park... until one wandered upon a stone that looked like none other, a portal into pre-human times when the west was wet and oozed with green. When dinosaur tails swung brawny and broad and rocks rolled 'round inside the belly.

I placed the gastrolith in the soft center of the horsehair nest I'd gathered three years before on that moki step hike. I couldn't stop looking at it. I rubbed my fingers over its smooth, glossy dimples as I kept repeating in my mind, *From the stomach of a dinosaur.* I held eons in the palm of my hand. It was the quintessential sign of continuity.

Sixty-Five

I wrote like a madwoman, chasing the almighty dollar. We'd made plans to go to an RV park on Lake Havasu for the winter when Jay's teaching semester was finished. There was a park on the California side at the end of a dead-end road, away from the lake's normal hubbub; friends said it was pretty wonderful. The first major snow came the night before we were to leave. Our electronic jacks were frozen to the ground. It took a blow torch to break loose.

We were three months on Lake Havasu. I learned to line-dance and rocked to the tunes of the local band, Old Spice, on Saturday nights. Jay rarely danced and never stayed long, leaving me to take the dance floor alone, bop and slow dance with men and women alike. How utterly terrific to be held without expectation, to laugh and move with others… to play with friends. I boogied my way back to myself.

I kayaked the lake's still waters and roamed the hills in search of birds. I photographed inlets, clouds and patterns on water. Jay took to riding his bike solo for several hours in the afternoon. We hiked the craggy, arid mountains packed with wild burros and played bocce ball with friends on Friday nights. To the outside world we were the ideal couple doing couple things, but laughter ceased within Tortuga's walls. Tempers flared as we struggled with the high highs and low lows. Sex-or-nothing led to no touching or intimacy. I ached for communication. Odd, flat, white warts appeared on my writing index finger.

We departed as spring draped the desert with lupine and poppies. We camped on the Painted Desert in Northern Arizona and continued east to Colorado, into the blinding sun. It was a relief to pull Tortuga into her Mancos resting place. Teak and Pooka beat a path to the door as we stepped outside into the welcome spring air. Within twenty minutes of landing, Jay said, "Christina... I want to stop RV'ing."

My blue eyes met his as I gulped for breath. "Stop... forever?" Here it was. The ultimatum.

"Yes," he said, "I'm tired. I want to stay put, live in one place."

From our first few years together I'd felt that the best thing about our relationship was that we didn't spend a lot of time processing, dumping feelings and analyzing actions, living through our tongues in a ceaseless chain of words. The last three years I'd realized that the worst thing about our relationship was that we didn't spend time processing, dumping feelings and analyzing actions.

"You need to stop writing and get a job," he said.

Stop writing? I would no more ask Jay to stop writing than I would ask him to stop breathing, yet here he was, asking me to do just that. He had already refused to read what I wrote; now he pinched my lifeline.

My mind spiraling, I went into survival mode. "I can't talk about this now." I grabbed the gastrolith and headed into the trees, simultaneously rubbing the stone between my fingers and wiping tears from my face. A white-breasted nuthatch swooped into the Narrow-Leaf Cottonwood and began her comic hop over the bark. Down the tree head first, peck, step sideways, peck peck, she followed a trail of hidden spiders and larvae through an undecipherable language of discovery.

I held the gastrolith against my chest. Unstoppable tears dripped upon my breasts, pooling salt-crust ponds upon the skin. And then, just like that, they stopped. My spirit lifted as I floated above the fray. Traveling mercies. I simultaneously touched the pain and beauty of every earthly spirit through the message of the gizzard stone: continuity. That was the message of hen turkey across the abyss and the procession of wild mothers that had come to me. Past, present and eternal converged.

Fifteen years with one person wrought tons of inertia. I still hoped to pull off a workable compromise. In the spirit of "gotta try everything," I found a part-time, seasonal job that allowed for a winter's break and time for writing. We gave up our South Dakota residency and became Coloradoans again. We were in the Colorado DMV getting our driver's licenses when Jay stepped up to get his eyes tested. The woman behind the machine had a sudden tone of worry in her voice as she requested that Jay repeat the drill. Jay didn't see objects to the side. He had absolutely no peripheral vision.

A follow-up appointment with an ophthalmologist confirmed that he had glaucoma. There was a reason he had missed seeing traffic and misjudged the shoulders of roads. No wonder he was irritable. Could this be why he drank more? This information was a game changer.

"My God, Christina," he said. "I'm sorry for the harsh words... all the anger. I didn't know. I didn't understand the pressure and stress." Jay held out his arms. We melted into tears. Together again.

But it didn't happen like that. He didn't talk; he didn't apologize. He expressed no regret for countless disrespectful scenes. I was sickened by the metaphor of glaucoma. No peripheral vision meant he only saw straight ahead. He lived a life with blinders, an unyielding man. It explained so much.

Louise Hay is a healer that I have often referred to for the psycho-spiritual basis for illness. I turned to her book. *Glaucoma: pressure from long-standing hurts. Stony unforgiveness.* I had my hunches as to what those hurts might entail as I envisioned him in Mass on his knees every Sunday. The piercing accuracy of the words was chilling. I shared Hay's information with Jay in a last-ditch hope.

He shrugged it off and mumbled a put-down.

I was done making deals.

Sixty-Six

I walked my slow way up one of my favorite mountain-rimmed drainages. Snow clung to the north side of the mountaintops; myriad beaver ponds dotted the stream that had only recently begun to flow. I was deep in thought, recounting the past few years and the miraculous scenes I had witnessed, the transmissions that had kept me astutely in the moment. I came to a spot where I had often stopped, and sat on a log, obedient to every sense. *Obedient*, from the Latin word *oboedire*, cognate to *ob-audire*, meaning *to listen, to hear* and by implication, *to act on what is heard*.

The chilly crystalline air enveloped me as the warm sun hit my flesh. A slight breeze swept my hair. The forest brimmed with the smell of spring. Water trembled down the creek, below the ice, with spring's first thaw. The resonance of nature soaked my body.

I closed my eyes and breathed as deeply as I could. This, the *real* world. The truth that came on nature's winds could not be manipulated. Wild places were essential for their candor, for the way they raised my vibrational level, healed my spirit and brought me into focus with one and all. In the midst of this pure, uncontrolled, oozing, life-giving life, they struck the mother-chord.

I usually turned around at this point, but I continued up the side of a mountain that led toward snow and an expansive view of the drainage below. I was hoping for a look at some elk caught unawares by an early visitor to their lands. Teak and I rounded the corner and the hair on her scruff stood on end. She let loose with a hearty bark and looked straight down the mountain. I followed her line of sight and jerked at the spectacle of a yearling mountain lion sixty feet below. The lion ran to the stream, leapt and disappeared on the other side into steep, thick woods.

My heart beat fast as I sought another glimpse. Then, just as quickly, another bark from Teak and another lion. This one followed the first. Then, another. It was mind-blowing. Three young lions had jumped the water. Then momma came into view.

She was magnificent. She was terrifying. She stared up at me and Teak. She could have been on us in an instant. I'd seen lions launch themselves from the power of their thick, long tail. I held Teak tight and stood dead still. The lioness did not take the route of her yearlings, instead she walked boldly upstream a few steps and stopped at a log that crossed the water. She jumped onto the log and was halfway across the stream when she looked back at me and let loose with a scream, keen fangs exposed. She continued to the other side, leapt off the log and disappeared.

Thunderstruck, I finally gulped for breath and took some steps that I might catch another glimpse. Four lions? No one sees four mountain lions at one time. I must have come upon a family that had been lazing on a south-facing slope. I headed for the nearest log and sat with Teak as my breath caught up with me.

Bare those teeth, Christina. Cross that stream.

Sixty-Seven

I remember when I first got wind of the RV life. A man in a chat room had commented, *You'd better darned well like the person you're with because you're going to sit across a small table and look at him every day.*

He was right, of course, but *like* was not enough. Much more important than like, or even love, was respect. There I was, sitting across from my husband, the man with whom I'd shared a quarter of my life. Memories swelled to the forefront: shared trips to Africa, conservation projects, book tours. There was love in wilderness cabins, naps in the pews of the Cathedral of Notre Dame, the resounding call of "Christina!" at climax. Our story, a mythological meeting across mountaintops, had been reduced to the dry bones of a dead zone. We were, in the words of Buddhist Saint Milarepa, a "Magnificent holy failure."

It was a Creatrix moment. No wonder those wild mothers came to me. In a deafening strum of the mother-chord, they presented their young. Whale, the soul of the sea. Puma, the soul of the mountain. Moose, griz and that loco turkey that took flight across the chasm. In an orgasm of potent alchemy, they had hijacked my soul. The message of those mothers was the destruction of home and subsequent extinction. The disappearance of the wild met the end of hope. The end of motherhood.

I had not offloaded my life into Tortuga that I might stall on a dead-end road. I was caught in the spiritual crosshairs, at the confluence of my personal soul and the soul of the planet. This was not only about Jay. A larger agenda loomed.

Soul knew. She created the conditions through which she needed to evolve and had plopped me down in front of wild eyes. I could no more stop the karmic plan than make my heart stop beating.

I sat down at the kitchen table, looked into Jay's blue eyes and told him I wanted a divorce.

I was leaving him for another woman. Me.

Sixty-Eight

When I thought of the spirit that had propelled me to shed my possessions and embark upon life in a motorhome, it went back to that little nut-brown girl from a farm in Iowa who stood topless in cowboy boots. Free and feral, I learned that risk with a twist of fear was a good thing. It was, in fact, the road to greatest pleasure.

I inhaled silence as the old moon crescent floated in the eastern sky. Veiled in clouds, it awaited the inevitable moment of sun, the new day that came not in a jerk of giant upheaval but a peaceful transition of power. The moon melted into daylight as I recalled one more meaning to the number seven. It was the counsel of native peoples to live on behalf of seven generations to come.

That waning moon was Creatrix-me. A silent revolution, if you will, as I journeyed from biological mother to spiritual mother of the planet. I would accept the mantle for the few years I had left on this phenomenal floating sphere. Mother whale, grizzly sow and I would pass on; not so the gastrolith, voice of cycads and dinosaurs. It was a sacred revelation that snuffed out loneliness and tended the restless soul. Home was the ever-holy place between precious ephemeral and exuberant continuity.

Sixty-Nine

Jay and I sold Tortuga five years from the day we pulled up roots in Taos and took to the road. We divorced within months. Her sale unleashed an avalanche of emotional energy. It marked the end of a miraculous dream, the purge of hearth. She had carried me, Jay, Belle, Teak and Pooka across the west from British Columbia to the tip of the Baja Peninsula, into high-altitude forests on Jeep roads, across vast expanses of desert and sky-fed plain to the edge of the sea. In a splash of perfect metaphor, she had never once had engine problems. I had stepped into my metal home and moved across the earth; she, in turn, had delivered me to the wild.

When the sale offer came I acted quickly. Creatrix at the helm, I purchased a 19-foot white travel trailer—aka woman wagon (thank you, Ole!) then bought a four-wheel drive pickup with a shell to pull the trailer. I made the exhausting transition from Tortuga to the trailer alone, sorting, packing and storing a few things with friends. I named the trailer La Perla. The Pearl. I loved her cozy layout. I walked in through the side door and to the left were the galley (booth and kitchenette) and the bathroom, complete with a little tub. A queen-sized bed, with a bona fide honest-to-goddess mattress, filled the space to the right. It was perfect... alone in bed was my favorite place to write. I tossed a potpourri of pillows onto the head of the bed and set the side table with candles, a picture of toddler Hope reaching for the sky, and the gastrolith. Then I hung a cursive exclamation made from unwound coat hangers by Babette: *Cowgirl Up!*

Jay and I agreed to divorce without lawyers. In short fits of heart, we managed to move beyond the marriage that had brought out the worst in us. "You are the essential woman," he said before he slipped into stony silence. Then Jay came down with a serious case of bronchitis. "Inflamed family environment," read Louise Hay. I kept the insight to myself.

We sat at our antique Formica table and worked out the details and splits of the divorce. I kept asking whether there was anything he wanted to say, ask... share. He said no, with that pursed lip of his. I apologized through tears for my contributions that had brought us to that point. As for Jay, no apologies. I rose from the table and we embraced a final time, his firm hand on the small of my back; then I turned and walked away.

In every hello is an inherent goodbye.

Seventy

I was Alaska-bound with Teak. A friend who had lived in Juneau for thirty-five years had suggested I visit; he was an avid fisherman and hunter. We would boat the untamed straits and seas known simply as "Southeast." I'd never been to Alaska. It was, in my mind, the epitome of the wild, the seamless next chapter in the saga of my soul.

Pooka would stay with Jay. I couldn't imagine her on the open sea, and he had the ideal living situation for a cat... an apartment in a barn with a cat door and infinite mice. On my final visit to say goodbye she met me at the truck, then high-tailed it for the door to the house. She wanted to go inside. She wanted both of us to go inside. *Not this time, Pooka. Never again.* Tears streamed as I lifted her silken spots to my face and kissed her. She hopped through tall grass as I drove away. *I'll be back for you*, I vowed.

I came to the highway and eased to a careful stop as I got the feel of the truck-trailer combo. Teak sat alertly in the back seat, hoping for a turn to the left and a round of fetch in the Mancos River. I twisted in my seat and rubbed her behind the ears. "Not today, Girl. We're heading for Alaska!" She cocked her head and looked at me with excited brown eyes. Three thousand miles beyond was Juneau, a rain forest island and unruly seas. I glanced at my hand on the wheel as I pulled out onto the highway.

The warts on my writing finger were gone.

Ominous thunderheads gathered on the western horizon as the sun climbed into my rearview mirror. The inside of my thigh quivered. *Sexy (almost) 60.* I smiled. I was one of those people-bubbles thrust from the dolphin blowhole, born into a brand new world.

Teak and me. A loft on wheels. Long brown hair and all.

Preview of
Soul Unzipped

Nature laid down one hell of a cathartic highway. Thunderheads roiled as Teak and I rolled northwest toward a distant Juneau. The dreamy wonder of passing panoramas was clearly under siege; my mind wouldn't shut up as rain, tears and memories mixed with fields of Colorado pinto beans and Moab's red rock canyons. Jay had called me "Essential Woman" during our final days together. When he uttered those words my eyes had welled with tears. Now that I was driving toward deliverance, I wondered whether that phrase had lit upon his brain before or after he had drained our joint account weeks earlier and precipitated the removal of my wedding ring. The cell phone chirped throughout the day as girlfriends checked-in. Emilie, Babette, Carole and daughter Hope—the gathering of the Sisters. The support only women provide.

I arrived in Price in the late afternoon, filled up with gas and began my descent into Salt Lake City. The plan was to park on the Lake for the night, to fall asleep amidst shorebirds and spacious darkness. This is when the deluge caught me. I white-knuckled the truck and trailer for twenty miles down steep mountain turns. Wind gusts and sheets of rain pummeled us. I would have pulled over but road construction had eliminated the shoulders and transformed pull-offs into bogs. The highway morphed into a flash-flood river, a hydro-plane waiting to happen. I put on the emergency blinkers and crawled, praying that no one would hit me from behind. It had taken five years of life on the road to force my hand, as I turned into the first flat safe place and took a breath. It was Wal-Mart, and I wasn't moving any further. I walked toward the large glass doors, past the frumpy smiling greeter and into the florescent-lit box. I grabbed a pint of Haagen Dazs Rum Raisin then bee-lined for La Perla. Tail-wagging Teak met me at the door as I closed the blinds, grabbed a spoon and climbed into my snuggly bed. The world was mine. All mine.

About the Author

Christina Nealson is author of three previous books: **New Mexico's Sanctuaries, Retreats and Sacred Places, Living on the Spine: A Woman's Life in the Sangre de Cristo Mountains** and **At the Edge: Cooperative Teachings for Global Survival.** She is the photographer for four others. The geo-gypsy and photojournalist has followed her heart and assignments to Africa, Central America and across the back roads of the U.S. West, Canada and Mexico. She teaches, lectures and blogs about the wild as she travels solo with Teak the chocolate lab and Hobo, an orange tabby who climbed onto the undercarriage of her truck in the British Columbia backwoods. Ultimately, she will tell you, that wildness begins within. You can visit her at christinanealson.com and read her latest ruminations and escapades at christinanealson.blogspot.com.

Acknowledgements

Spirited gratitude to my community of heart and mind… those who read, commented and came through with whatever it took on behalf of my words: Elizabeth Hanly, Babette Kimble, Kizzen Lakai, Carole Summer. Thank you Debora Lewis, cover designer and format Goddess, I owe you a widow-maker burger; Emilie Vardaman for your invaluable edits; Harvey Stanbrough for the polish. Thank you precious daughter, Hope Nealson.

Thank you Johanna Smith for sharing your toothbrush in Yuma; and Philip Walters for all those hours on your back on my kitchen floor… wiring my solar panels.

Thanks to the anonymous man who snapped the cover shot on one glorious day at Avalanche Lake in Glacier National Park. I set it up, handed you the camera and asked for your name, "just in case it ends up as the cover." You laughed and said not necessary. I hope you liked the shots I took of you.

Gratefulness to the generous, rowdy, tear-jerking, sassy, insightful, perverted, pugnacious, captivating, heart-wrenching, soul-expanding myriad friends and strangers along the road. You know who you are.

Thank you Jon Bush, who landed a swift kick (and a bottle of Tanqueray) just when I needed it.

I owe my being to the Wild Ones, for infusing my life with mystery, fury and instinct. You are, as Alice Walker so aptly states, my spiritual equivalent to oxygen.

Words of Praise for Christina Nealson

Living on the Spine
A Woman's Life in the Sangre de Cristo Mountains

"Christina Nealson is the West's answer to Annie Dillard, yet Nealson's voice is so authentically her own. This is a book of eloquent witness to questions that cannot be answered, only lived." —Julia Cameron, author of **The Artist's Way**

"Her work is not a linear portrayal of facts but rather a poetic and reflective glimpse of a heart and soul. It is gentle, gracious, and profound." —**Library Journal**

"If you dare to nourish yourself with a woman's truth, the colors of solitude, and Nature's randy humor—grab this book, take it home, and go to bed with it. I guarantee satisfaction!" —Susan S. Weed, author of **Healing Wise**

"Christina's achingly beautiful descriptions bring the Sangre de Cristo landscape to life. Her knife-edged imagery cuts through pretension and emotional detachment, leading us into a sumptuous, sometimes violent wilderness." —Stephen R. Jones, coauthor of **The Shortgrass Prairie**

"Christina's words are fresh and clear as the water of a high mountain spring; deep and warming as the cave of a winter bear first-suckling her naked young." —Brooke Medicine Eagle, native Earthkeeper and ceremonial leader, author of **Buffalo Woman Comes Singing**

Drive Me Wild
A Western Odyssey

"Drive Me Wild is an odyssey about the wonders of this planet, the vicissitudes of a marriage, the wild heart of many places. It is a mixture of great joys and deep sorrows. There are whales, dolphins, mountain lions, moose, sea turtles and grizzly bears... even a miraculous gastrolith! This is a lovely book, a lyrical disquisition on a very complex journey, told in simple and crystal-clear prose. It is crammed full of delights, beautiful country and sudden little miracles. Diamonds of experience and information glitter on every page. The book is a paean to wanderers. Turn in your badge, Jack Kerouac, there's a new sheriff in town and her name is Christina Nealson." —John Nichols, author of **The Milagro Beanfield War** and **On Top of Spoon Mountain**

"This book's a wild ride, a deep story, a journey that will open your heart and prompt your soul to speak. It's not easy, but no real journey is. It is beautiful and funny, scary and sad, honest and compelling. It pairs words we often think of as antithetical: 'motorhome' with 'enlightenment,' 'aging' with 'power.' Read it and be swept away." —Susan Tweit, author of **Walking Nature Home: A Life's Journey**

"A full-time RVers mantra is 'one thing in, one thing out.' That becomes Christina Nealson's Zen mantra as she pares down to the bare essentials in her life. RVing is not only a vehicle for her travels where she lyrically describes her experiences with nature and encounters with wildlife, but is also a metaphor for her spiritual journey of the soul. **Drive Me Wild** made me long for those quiet spots off the beaten path and the beauty of wild places—a must-read for the RVer on a spiritual path." —Jaimie Hall Bruzenak, author of **RV Traveling Tales: Women's Journeys on the Open Road**

"Get in, buckle up and hang on! Reminiscent of Steinbeck's **Travels with Charley** and Least Heat Moon's **Blue Highways,** Christina weaves wilderness and personal reflection with the courage of a bruja and the sensibilities of the curandera. The story of this slice of life is told in simple, profound language that entices one to sit on the dashboard of Tortuga-the-motorhome and wonder what comes next in this gypsy life. The book is not about RV travels, though Tortuga has her own life. Christina relates the journey of the captain and co-captain in a bold, captivating story that takes one deeply and wondrously into freedom life on the road, a place we all long to be."
—Dr. Roger Strachan, Director, Center for Creative Choice and Wilderness Encounter

"Can the freedom of the open road and the solace of wild places heal a tottering, claustrophobic romance? Interweaving mesmerizing descriptions of encounters with whales, grizzly bears, mountain lions, and glowing wilderness with frank talk about independent spirits struggling to connect, Christina Nealson takes us on a roller coaster ride into the wildest reaches of the American West and the heart of a complex relationship." —Stephen Jones, author of **The Last Prairie** and **Peterson Field Guides: The North American Prairie**

CPSIA information can be obtained at www.ICGtesting.com
Printed in the USA
LVOW101819191212

312454LV00019B/813/P